Barbara Matthews

GARDENS OF NEW ZEALAND

ACKNOWLEDGEMENT

Many people have been involved in the making of this book —
owners of gardens large and small who have allowed photographs
to be taken of their gardens, and those who have provided
information of an historic nature. To all these good friends, sincere
thanks. Special mention must be made of Julian who contributed
most of the photographs.

Published by Weldon Publishing Ltd
    Suite C, 500 Parnell Road, Parnell
    Auckland, New Zealand

© Barbara Matthews 1983

First published 1983, reprinted 1988

Photography: Barbara Matthews, Julian Matthews

Design: Suellen Allen

Editor: Chris O'Brien

Typesetting: Auckland Typographic Services Ltd, Auckland

Printing: Kyodo Printing Co. Ltd, Singapore

ISBN 0-86866-073-6

Barbara Matthews

GARDENS OF NEW ZEALAND

Lansdowne Press
Auckland Sydney London New York

foreword

The Rt. Hon. Sir John Marshall, GBE, CH.

Nearly everyone in New Zealand has a garden. We find it satisfying to feel the good earth in our hands, to watch the miracle of growth and to follow the changing seasons in the flowers and the leaves. This is part of the New Zealand way of life. It is a good life.

For those who do not have their own plot of ground there are public gardens and parks and innumerable beds of flowers and shrubs filling odd corners in the streets of our towns and in the countryside.

Our country is a good place for gardens. It is surrounded by temperate seas which encourage a comfortable climate. The warm sun and the gentle rain conspire together to make the earth a responsive seed bed. For years beyond memory unique New Zealand trees and plants have flourished and renewed themselves from generation to generation in splendid isolation.

Then two hundred years ago an invasion began which has brought to our land a lavish profusion of trees and flowers from every continent. The Maori had gardens before the Europeans came, but the white settlers had a varied and cultivated world to draw upon. This they did and we, their decendants, are today the beneficiaries of this bountiful heritage.

This in a few words is the story which Barbara Matthews tells in this book: the way our gardens began, round the colonial cottage and the bush homestead, the way they developed over the years in the multitude of small home gardens, in the notable private estates, in the private parks, in towns and cities, in the reserves and plantations.

Mrs Matthews is qualified by a lifetime of gardening and study and research to write with authority, as she has been doing in numerous publications for many years. To collect the material for this book she has travelled thousands of kilometres throughout New Zealand, interviewed hundreds of people, pursued elusive facts through many books and papers, visited almost all the places about which she has written and taken innumerable photographs from which to illustrate the text.

The result is a unique book giving for the first time a concise and authoritative account of New Zealand gardens and gardening, their origins, their history, their growth and development and their present status. It is a fascinating story.

John Marshall

CONTENTS

the beginnings   8

land of contrasts   24

old farm gardens   38

larger gardens take shape   60

everyman's garden   82

native plants in the garden   114

gardens for the people   132

places to visit   148

the beginnings

Long before the first Europeans set foot in New Zealand, gardens were made by the Maori people, who brought with them on their great migrations seeds and roots of the plants that had sustained them in Polynesia. They cultivated large areas of land, mainly in the north where it was warmer, and grew crops of kumara (sweet potato), hue (gourds) which provided them with food vessels, taro, yam, and though not so successfully, the paper mulberry, from the inner bark of which, tapa cloth was made. The kumara, which was introduced even before the great migration of the fourteenth century, is still an important vegetable in New Zealand. The taro is occasionally grown in the northern areas, and the Maori gourd has in recent times been rescued from oblivion to be grown and carved with Maori motifs and used as an article of artistic interest.

Sir Joseph Banks, the first director of the Royal Botanic Gardens, Kew, who in 1770 accompanied Captain James Cook on the *Endeavour* and financed the botanical exploration on that expedition, took note of the way the Maori people made their gardens. After landing at Tolaga Bay on the East Coast of the North Island, he remarked, "They certainly have excellent vegetables . . . so well was the ground till'd, that I have seldom seen . . . land better broke down . . . in them were planted sweet potatoes, Cocos (taro) and some of the cucumber kind" (the hue or gourd). Describing the gardens, ". . . laid out in rows, others . . . all laid by a line most regularly; the cucumbers set in small hollows or dishes, such as we do in England. There were plantations from 1 or 10 acres each in the Bay . . . might be 160 to 200 acres in cultivation . . . each distinct patch was fenced in with reeds placed close one by another, so that scarce a mouse could creep through."[1]

When Banks saw the land, the Maori had been cultivating it for centuries and were skilled horticulturists with a knowledge of plants which they put to many uses. But their interest was not confined to edibles. Banks noted the beautiful kakabeak, *Clianthus puniceus,* growing about their dwellings, and added it to his botanical specimens.

Banks and his assistant botanist, Dr Solander, were leading naturalists of the age. They found New Zealand a wonderland of endemic plants – species that were unknown in any other country of the world. They returned to England with many botanical specimens and seeds, but not plants because of the difficulties in transporting them successfully.

On Cook's second voyage Banks was replaced by the Forsters, father and son, who collected botanical specimens and wrote a paper on the economic possibilities of the fibres of native flax or *Phormium.* The paper was read by a scientist named Labillardière, who accompanied the de Surville expedition of 1791 when it called in at Doubtful Sound just long enough for him to gather some of these plants, which he successfully transported to France. They were rooted at Le Jardin des Plantes in Paris and eventually found their way to many gardens throughout Europe. After the first explorers, whalers and sealers were frequent visitors to New Zealand and some set up stations and trading posts in which flax became an important commodity.

It is almost certain that by the end of the eighteenth century more New Zealand plants were growing in Great Britain than were European plants in the new land. Yet the exchange had started. Cook was the first person to attempt a garden in the European style when on his second voyage, in 1773, he stayed awhile at Dusky Sound. The puggy, red soil in this area of high rainfall was not likely to be productive, but Cook set fire to a covering of wood to dry out the topsoil which his men "dug up, and sowed with several sorts of garden seeds. The soil was such as did not

2

Opposite Page. *Kemp House at Kerikeri is the oldest house in New Zealand, made of pit-sawn kauri and erected by the skilled craftsmen who were a very important part of the missionary community. It was first occupied by the Rev. John Butler who was responsible for planting the first fruit trees and vegetables. Butler was succeeded by a blacksmith, James Kemp, who joined the Society as a lay missionary; he and his family occupied the house until 1974 when it was given by Mr Ernest Kemp to the Historic Places Trust which continues to administer it for the nation.*
Beside the front door, the lamp that was used by the missionaries to guide boats to the landing stage, still glows.

2. *The early explorers found in the New Zealand bush a wonderland of plants previously unknown to the Europeans.*

A staghorn fern frames the Kemp House garden, always bright with old-fashioned flowers; some of the original
plants or their progeny, such as the wisteria over the door and an old pink rose, remain.
When the house was taken over by the Historic Places Trust, the roof was retiled and the garden carefully restored and retained, as far as possible as originally planned. But a flash flood in 1982 largely demolished the garden and it will take some time to re-establish the lost trees and hedges. There is a charming story that Mrs James Kemp sowed some sweet orange pips from fruit she collected on the passage out; two grew into trees and one survived for 100 years.

Opposite page. *Kemp House with the old Anglican Church in the background.*

promise success to the planter; it was, however, the best we could find."[2] This was April, the time of early spring in England, but it was the beginning of a long, wet winter in Dusky Sound. There is no evidence that any of the seeds survived.

Later that year another garden was made, on Motuara Island in Queen Charlotte Sound by the master and some of the men from the *Adventure,* which accompanied Cook's barque *Resolution* on the expedition.

Potatoes, turnips, carrots and parsnips were planted on an unoccupied pa site, and left to the care and benefit of the natives. When Cook returned on his third voyage, however, he recorded that "not the least vestige of these now remained." Yet he went on to say "at all the other gardens then planted by Captain Furneaux (who commanded the *Adventure),* although now wholly overrun with the weeds of the country, we found cabbages, onions, leeks, purslane, radishes, mustard and a few potatoes. These potatoes, which were first brought from the Cape of Good Hope, had been greatly improved by change of soil and, with proper cultivation, would be superior to those produced in most other countries. Though the New Zealanders are fond of this root, it was evident that they had not taken the trouble to plant a single one (much less any of the articles which we had introduced), and if it were not for the difficulty of clearing the ground where potatoes had once been planted, there would not have been any now remaining."[3] Nevertheless Colenso records that Captain Cook on his 1769 journey around the southernmost tip of the North Island gave seeds, pigs and fowls to a native chief, Tuanui, and "from some of these garden seeds sprang the 'Maori cabbage' of the coast, which . . . grew very thickly there and over on to Palliser Bay and often served me, when travelling, for breakfast." He further remarked that "they were a great benefit to them and still extensively used by the natives".[4]

Although Cook's efforts to introduce the Maori to a more varied diet met with little success, a more determined effort was made by the Rev. Samuel Marsden (who was responsible for the establishment of the Church Missionary Society and its settlements in New Zealand). He was so convinced that the Maori needed to be converted not only to Christianity but also to the European way of agriculture, that he selected as his first missionaries, skilled artisans who also had a good practical knowledge of farming and gardening.

Landing at the Bay of Islands, the missionaries of the Society made their first settlement at Rangihoua where they were under the protection of a friendly chief, Ruatara. They endured considerable privations at first, and the soil did not encourage them to grow much in the way of food crops or flowers. Many more missionaries and workmen followed in 1819 and brought useful plants, seeds and roots from Marsden's farm at Parramatta.

It was an important year in the history of New Zealand for several reasons. Marsden chose Kerikeri as the second site for a settlement, and the Rev. John Butler, who was in charge of the Mission, planted the first known orchard, consisting of grape vines and 185 fruit trees – apples, pears, plums, peaches and citrus. Some of these survive still and continue to bear well.

The site was a strategic one, even if a little too close to Hongi Hika's pa when the influential chief rebelled in the years that followed. Here was a beautiful tidal basin where Hongi's war canoes lay hidden at the ready (and pleasure craft were to lie at anchor in the future). But the soil was very fertile and the climate mild; there was also plenty of wood available for buildings.

Butler and a schoolteacher, the missionary blacksmith James Kemp and carpenters with their wives and children, moved into temporary dwellings while houses were being erected.

The Mission House was finished in 1822 and Butler moved in with his family, but he left the Mission in New Zealand in 1823, and the missionary-blacksmith, James Kemp, took up residence there. His family eventually purchased the Mission House and it became the home of succeeding generations for 142 years. A welcoming lamp by the front door has been kept constantly alight since the days when it was needed to guide the missionaries home on dark and perilous nights. Also known as Kemp House, it is the oldest building erected by Europeans in New Zealand.

Nearby, the stone store, almost as historic, stands as a reminder of unsettled days. Of local materials, it was built in 1832 as a fireproof building for the missionaries to store their goods. Bishop Selwyn used part of it as a library when he was stationed at Waimate. In 1974 the grandson of James Kemp presented the buildings to the New Zealand Historic Places Trust.

The Mission site is a source of great attraction to visitors; it has been preserved and still retains the character of a bygone age. The little church on the hill, the orchard and the trees planted by Butler remain, if overgrown, as does the old-fashioned garden, recently reduced in a sudden flood of the lovely river which swept away some of the frontage of the Mission house. No other mission settlement has been preserved so well, but several others have been restored, notably at Waimate, which was later to become known as Waimate North.

2

Opposite page. Rosa gallica versicolor *'Rosa Mundi'*.

2.   *The old stone store at Kerikeri was built in 1832 as a store and refuge for the missionaries. Today it houses artefacts and reminders of those early days.*

The Roman Catholic Mission arrived to establish its faith in 1838, but there are no sites as historic and as notable for their gardens as the settlements made by the Anglicans. However, at Russell (formerly Kororareka), Bishop Pompallier left his mark in what is one of the most elegant buildings and beautiful gardens in the area.

The Rev. William Williams, brother of the Rev. Henry Williams, arrived with his wife in 1826 and made a garden at the third Mission settlement at Paihia. He planted a good vegetable garden and also the pip of a lemon tree which survived until recent times. Their cottage was described by Mrs Maunsell, wife of the Rev. Robert Maunsell who succeeded to the place when they came from England in 1835, "a pretty cottage, a verandah in front through the trelliswork of which woodbines and roses most luxuriantly twine. What we consider beautiful roses in England grow here almost as weeds. There is a large garden in front, out-building and orchard at back . . . the choicest vegetables grow here in abundance . . . peaches by loads, quinces, apples, mulberries, greens, asparagus, cauliflower . . .".[5]

Peaches especially flourished; almost every stone that was thrown to the ground grew. Credit is usually given the missionaries for the quick establishment of this fruit tree around every Maori pa and European settlement in the northern areas, but it is very likely that they were grown by the Maori long before this. One of the earliest visitors to our northern shores was Crozet, a botanist on the expedition of Marion du Fresne who was massacred at the Bay of Islands in 1772. He recorded that wherever he set foot he sowed stones, pips and seeds which he collected at the Cape of Good Hope during his voyage. These would certainly have included peaches, so that the Maori knew of, and probably propagated them, before the arrival of the missionaries.[6]

No tree reminded the missionaries of home as much as the oak. An oak which in 1824 was planted in Paihia by missionary Richard Davis of the Church Missionary Society, and which was later removed to Waimate where the Society has established a farm, stands to this day. Another, grown from an acorn planted at Ashwell's Mission Station near Taupiri, was planted by Bishop Selwyn in 1840 and is said to be the oldest oak in the Waikato. It was the forerunner of many other oaks and 'English' trees for which this area is noted. Ashwell's had a well-kept flower garden fragrant with the scent of roses, but although the site is marked no sign of the garden remains. However, at Selwyn Road in Te Awamutu, the garden of the Otawhao Mission, established in 1839, is commemorated by a public park.

That the missionaries were interested in planting trees is evident from specimens that remain on the sites of the early missions. At Tauranga in the Bay of Plenty, the first mission station, established in 1835 by the Ven. Archdeacon A. N. Brown, had an interesting garden which has been maintained by his descendants as far as possible in its original state. The trees have grown immensely, but only one of the original Norfolk Island pines planted in the area remains. So fast-growing were they that they were used as landmarks by the sailing ships which until the early twentieth century made their way to harbour at Tauranga. Copper beech, oak, bunya bunya pines and palms are strange companions planted together in this garden with the tree ferns, kauri, pohutukawa and kowhai.

These native trees in particular were loved by the early missionaries, who often planted them around their homes. At Grove Cottage in Waimate North the missionary George Clarke planted groves of native trees as well as avenues of oaks.

His home was razed in the Maori war of the 1840s when the Mission was abandoned, but the Mission House itself and the Church were spared. The Mission House was one of the first places to be restored by the Historic Places Trust soon after it came into being in 1954. It is the second oldest surviving house in the country. With its typical colonial verandah and dormer windows it is a very graceful building surrounded by fine old eucalyptus trees, magnolias, ficus and an old-fashioned flower garden. The oaks beside the church and about the graveyard were planted by George Clarke.

Opposite page and 2. *Pompallier House, Russell was named for and commemorates Bishop Pompallier, the first Roman Catholic Bishop of the south-west Pacific who established the first R.C. Mission at Kororareka (Russell). His own house was actually on the waterfront, but he built a two-storey pise-de-terre (rammed mud) house to accommodate a printing press to produce religious books in Maori. The building escaped the sacking of the town by Hone Heke but in 1856 the Bishop removed the Mission and presses to Auckland. It was rescued from decay and remodelled in 1877, the remains of the original building being enclosed in the beautifully designed wooden structure which stands as Pompallier House today. Part of the interior has been removed to show the original pise construction and relics of the early mission and the original printing press are housed here.*

3. *The establishment of a mission station at Tauranga followed the decision of the Church Missionary Society in the early 1830s to expand its operations south of the Bay of Islands. With its large Maori population and excellent harbour, Tauranga became a desirable site and by 1835 the Te Papa Mission was in operation. Norfolk Island pines were planted by the resident missionary, Archdeacon Alfred Brown, which for many years were used as guiding landmarks for sailing ships entering the harbour.*

The Waimate North church dates from 1872 but the mission had already been established for over 40 years. Old oaks, a feature of the site, were planted by missionaires soon after their arrival. When Charles Darwin visited Waimate in 1835 he wrote in delighted approval, "An enchanter's wand!"

For all their tribulations the influence of the early missionaries spread, and by the 1830s a mellow note crept into the records of their lives, reflecting their joy in their gardens and the natural things about them. Visitors from the outside world often included leading naturalists and plant explorers, names that were to become famous in the annals of history.

Charles Darwin, who in December 1835 called in at the Bay of Islands during his world voyage on the *Beagle,* remarked in his journal on the cottages of the missionaries at Paihia. "It was quite pleasing to behold the English flowers in the gardens before the houses; there were roses of several kinds, and honeysuckle, jessamine, stocks, and whole hedges of sweet briar." When he visited the Waimate Mission Station, he was so astonished at what they had achieved in five years that, "I cannot attempt to describe all I saw; there were gardens with every fruit and vegetable which England produces and many belonging to a warmer climate . . . gorse for fences and English oaks, and many kinds of flowers."

Gorse was to become a noxious weed, the briar and other roses grew so well in the warm climate that they escaped into the countryside and grew wild there. The old, old-fashioned roses with delightful French names, gallicas and damasks, moss and musk roses, most-loved of the earliest garden flowers and sought-after by collectors in modern times, have been found in the vicinity of the old settlements and restored to gardens.

Many of the other plants, described in the letters of the missionaries' wives and the works of early writers, also became garden escapes. There was the blackberry (intended as a fruiting vine), herbs like borage and chicory, teasels to facilitate the combing of sheep's wool, the arum and montbretia bulbs from the Cape, and the dock which was seen by Darwin, causing him to comment, "The common dock is widely disseminated and will, I fear, for ever remain a proof of the rascality of an Englishman, who sold the seeds for those of the tobacco plant." Many other plants that were to take kindly to their new environment were also to pose problems to farmers and gardeners in the future.

Another of the great botanists to visit New Zealand in 1841 was Dr. Joseph Dalton Hooker, (later Sir Joseph) who adds further interesting information to that recorded by Darwin. He met and formed a lasting and important friendship with William Colenso, who took him on botanical excursions in the area of Kerikeri.

Travelling by canoe up the Waikare Inlet, Hooker admired the lovely *Pomaderris kumerahou,* golden tainui, coming into flower. Leaving the river at the Rev. C. Baker's property, he noted that Baker had in one season gathered 1000 bushels of peaches from the trees around the house, while Cape gooseberries covered the ground to a great extent in places.

In their first few years, much bravery, determination and dedication was required on the part of the missionaries, and it is easy to imagine their disappointment and frustration when rebellious natives at Paihia tore up their carefully made gardens and destroyed their homes. A mission station at Whangaroa, established in 1826 by the Wesleyans, was producing good crops of vegetables when it was destroyed "by a marauding band of Hongi's warriors who no sooner arrived at the plantations than they began their work of devastation in pulling up the kumara, corn etc. which were just above the ground. In the early potatoes, which they bartered with the whalers for firearms, they found a booty."[7] The missionaries had built solid houses, had enclosed their gardens with stout fences, and were proud of their four-acre wheatfield, but the Maori chief returned with his men and completely razed the station.

In 1883, the Rev. William Williams introduced Christianity on the East Coast of the North Island, spreading the faith by distributing the Bible in the Maori language, in which he was an expert. He came to Turanga to establish a mission station, and when his house was built he ensured that he would have a garden by sending to an established trader at Turanga a collection of fruit trees to be grown in his care until his arrival. He listed "Peach 12, Nectarine 4, Apricot 4, Plum 8, Apple 14, Cherry 4, Pear 4, Walnut 2".[8]

2

3

Opposite page. *Many of the plants introduced by early missionaries and settlers for their gardens soon escaped to become naturalised in the wild. Herbs like borage and chicory were favourites; blackberry was planted for its fruit, and these teasels intended to facilitate the combing of sheep's wool.*

2. The native kumerahou or golden tainui, much admired by the botanist Joseph Hooker as he ventured up the Waikare Inlet in the Bay of Islands in 1841.

3. Gorse, introduced by the missionaries and continued by early nurserymen as a hedging plant, spread all over the countryside, clothing the hills in golden swathes in early spring.

When the Hauhau wars reached Poverty Bay Williams had no choice but to leave for Napier, returning later to find home and garden horribly wrecked. In 1867 he and his wife decided to live in Napier and built a new home at Hakarere in 1867. He was by then Bishop of Waiapu. Together they spent a settling-in period "largely concerned with planting out oak trees and shrubs which had been bedded out at Napier and the Bay of Islands ever since the evacuation of Waerenga-a-Hika (at Poverty Bay)." The Williams made at least six gardens during their years of service to the Church and the education of the Maori. In his last days, in 1876, "he was able to potter about his rose and fuchsia garden which was his particular joy".

The exotics, or introduced plants, grown by the missionaries had been acquired when they broke the long journey from the northern hemisphere at Capetown, South Africa, or at Sydney, Australia.[9] They had no success in transporting living plants on the six-month voyage through the humid heat of the tropics. The problems of preserving seeds had been overcome by various methods, such as placing them in melted bees-wax in metal containers. Hardwood cuttings such as those of roses and the budwood of fruit trees were placed in airtight metal cases lined with moss. Explorers returning with living plants met with the same difficulties and had little luck. In the case of Labillardière's flax however, its strong constitution apparently enabled it to survive the extremes. It was a frustrating situation, but quite suddenly there was a remarkable but simple discovery which solved these problems.

Opposite page. *The herb garden in the kitchen area of the Waitangi Treaty House creates a feeling of old-world enchantment.*

2. *The giant white arum lily was among the first bulbous plants brought from South Africa by the settlers who stopped at Capetown on their way. It soon naturalised in the north and spread to all the milder coastal areas becoming a nuisance to farmers. Today it is still popular in gardens because it flowers in winter.*

3. *Old rose* 'Cardinal De Richelieu'

A new technique was discovered by a Dr Nathaniel Ward, a medical practitioner who was a keen observer of nature. He found that plants would live under the most variable of conditions without any attention if they were grown in a moist, enclosed atmosphere such as that of a bottle. He was a friend of Sir William Hooker who succeeded Banks as director at Kew, and he also knew of the world voyage of Mr Vancouver, who, with the botanist Menzies, came to New Zealand in 1791 in search of new materials. The failure of this expedition to bring live plants home from far-away lands interested the doctor and must have provided him with a challenge. He set to work to overcome the problem, and in 1833 he produced two glass cases like miniature glasshouses, strengthened at the sides and corners and hermetically sealed to insulate plants against climatic changes and extremes. He filled the bottom of the cases with damp soil, planted ferns and grasses in them, and sent them off to Sydney on the deck of a sailing ship. The trial proved successful and the cases were returned to England containing some Australian plants which withstood a journey around Cape Horn and across the tropics, even continuing to grow in spite of all the difficulties which had baffled the best scientific brains.

This apparently simple but great invention, which was named the Wardian case, made possible the exchange of plants throughout the world. It was the beginning of a new era for the plant explorers who had been bringing out of the jungles and mountains of Asia, the Americas, India, and the Antipodes, the most fantastic plants to satisfy the demands of the eager owners of glasshouses and gardens in Europe, only to lose most of them in the final stages of transportation.

One of the first people to bring plants from England to New Zealand was a young gardener named John Edgerley. He came to the new country in 1836 to work for Lieut. Thomas McDonnell, who retired from the Royal Navy and bought a shipbuilding yard at Horeke near Hokianga. Edgerley made a lovely garden for him at his home but credit is given to McDonnell for bringing to New Zealand the first Norfolk Island pine seeds. As Norfolk Island was often visited by passing ships it is likely that seed reached New Zealand before this, and one tree which still stands at Wapahu, Bay of Islands, was said to have been planted as early as 1828 by Gilbert Mair, an early settler and trader. He later farmed at Whangarei, where he is commerated by Mair Park, noted for its native trees, and rose garden.

Edgerley was a keen plantsman. He served his time with McDonnell and returned to England with the one objective of bringing back by the new method of transport as many plants and seeds as possible. He returned about 1842 and he set up a nursery in Auckland where he grew such new species as *Magnolia grandiflora* from North America and deciduous magnolias and camellias, jacarandas, and many other exotic trees and shrubs from far-off lands. Some of the first of these he gave to his friends, including the missionaries. The journals of the Rev. William Williams mention a visit to Edgerley in Auckland in 1843 but there is unfortunately little information to prove that he was responsible for the widespread distribution of many of the fine old trees which are such a feature of the Auckland region today. He was the forerunner of other keen plantsmen, nurserymen and gardeners who came with the flood of settlers after the Treaty of Waitangi in 1840 and who were to shape the pattern of New Zealand gardens as we know them today.

Opposite page. Jacaranda was one of the first of the South American trees to be grown extensively in the warmer parts of New Zealand.

2. *Among the most favoured trees were the camellias, and specimens planted by the missionaries are still to be seen in the north.*

3. Magnolia grandiflora, *an early introduction in the north.*

1. Sir Joseph Banks, in his journals, reported seeing a few tapa growing in the Bay of Islands, "but they were poor specimens." *Sir Joseph Banks in New Zealand,* from his Journals, edited by W.P. Morrel (Reed).

2, 3. From the Journals of Sir Joseph Banks, in *Captain Cook in New Zealand.* H. Reed (A.H. & A. W. Reed).

4. Colenso made regular journerys from Hawke's Bay to the Wairarapa, Wellington and the far north twice a year, walking through these rugged parts of the country on his way to the Ahuriri Mission. *William Colenso,* A.G. Bagnall and C.G. Paterson (taken from the Transactions of the New Zealand Institute, No. 10.)

5. *The Women of New Zealand,* Helen Simpson, (N.Z. Department of Internal Affairs).

6. "I sowed stones and pips wherever I went, on the plains, in the glens, on the slopes and even on the hills." H. Guthrie Smith used this quotation by Crozet in his book, *Sorrows and Joys of a New Zealand Naturalist.* He expressed his amazement that "authority without exception agrees in ascribing the earliest peaches to missionary enterprise. Sown with the most elementary sense of choice they could not but have sprouted and peaches especially borne fruit in quantity in the third and even the second year."

7. *The Story of Northland,* H. Reed, (A.H. & A.W. Reed).

8. *The Turanga Journals,* edited by Francis Porter. (Price Milburn/ Victoria University Press).

9. "Those settlers who came out in the ships touching at the Cape generally brought supplies of flowers and shrubs from there and they all do uncommonly well . . ." Charlotte Godley in her *Letters from Early New Zealand,* 1850-53, quoted by S. Challenger in *Changes in the Canterbury Landscape,* Annual Journal of the Royal NZ Institute of Horticulture, 1974.

land of contrasts

The gardens of New Zealand have not as yet evolved a distinctly national character as have those in lands with established cultures, but the plants grown in them are the best of two hemispheres, and if any distinct pattern emerges it will be derived from the use of these contrasting materials, the evergreen natives and the exotic, the hardy and the tender.

Cold climate plants, particularly deciduous species, thrive best in the southern areas where the early settlements were largely made by immigrants from England and Scotland, and the garden traditions brought by the pioneers remain firmly implanted. But as one goes north this conservatism gives way to more freedom of expression in landscaping, encouraged by the wider range of plants that can be grown so easily. Indigenous species grow beside those from all over the world, kowhai and flax with hibiscus and jacaranda.

The interesting differences in the gardens of the various regions of the country are largely the result of the climate and the weather. Taken collectively, one could say that they reflect a land of vast contrasts such as is found in no other country of comparable size. "New Zealand is a land of infinite variety. In no other part of the globe is there to be found, in so limited an area, such a diversity of natural features. The snowy heights of the Himalayas, the glaciers and fiords of Norway, the geysers and volcanoes of America and Iceland, the grassy steppes of Russia, the forest-clad hills of tropical Brazil and sub-Antarctic Chile, all have their counterparts in the *multum in parvo* of the South Pacific."[1]

It fascinated an English traveller, J. Robertson-Scott, founder-editor of *The Countryman,* a famous periodical, who described it more succinctly as "a Pocket World."

The climate varies from humid sub-tropical to alpine, from heavy rainfall on the West Coast of the South Island to the dry, hot and cold extremes of an almost continental climate in Central Otago and South Canterbury and the central plateau of North Island. Where least expected, there exist micro-climates — localities where the temperatures are quite different to those generally experienced in a region or one area of it. Such places offer exciting opportunities for gardening. Every area has its advantages and its limitations.

To understand the nature of the gardens it is necessary to comprehend a little of the distinctive natural features of Aotearoa, this 'Land of the Long White Cloud,' stretching for over 1700 kilometres from Cape Reinga in the farthest north to Stewart Island, a green gem at the southernmost tip. The sea can be seen on either coast from almost any high point of the spinal ranges which divide the length of the land into two distinct climates — the Tasman sea, driven by the prevailing winds, beating on the western shores and the great Pacific rolling in on the east. The mountains, not quite as dominant in the North Island as in the South where the alps are clad in eternal snow, influence the weather by interrupting the westerly winds, causing them to drop their rains, and thus providing the contrast and variation between east and west.

2

3

The New Zealand climate varies from humid sub-tropical to alpine, from the heavy rainfall of the West Coast to the dry, hot and cold extremes of Central Otago and the North Island's volcanic plateau.

2. Raoulias, lichens and tiny alpine flowers hug the stones and boulders of the dry Marlborough high country.

3. Ice-plants and grasses, native and introduced, are used to control the movement of windswept drifting sands.

Opposite page. *An old cottage, restored and repainted, sits invitingly at the edge of the native forest. The mature apple tree, adorned by spring blossom lends an air of peaceful contrast.*

2

3

Opposite page. *Luxuriant beech forest typical of high rainfall areas such as Westland and the southern half of the North Island.*

2. *Mosses of every colour and texture thrive in the constant dampness in the vicinity of the Wilmot Pass, Fiordland.*

3. *A field of tulips stretches to the horizon. Hardy bulbs are grown commercially in the centre of the North Island and Southland, looking just like the fields of Holland in springtime.*

The vagaries of the weather is one of the outstanding features of regional gardening in New Zealand. Auckland alone spreads itself not at the foot of mountains but on the bumps of extinct volcanic craters, so that gardening in this region is complicated by scoria outcrops.

However, with Northland, it is the warmest and most humid part of the country, ideal for sub-tropical plants. The hibiscus, the orange and the lemon are common sights.

The early settlers must have been confused at first by the absence of the distinct definition which marked the seasons in their homelands. Autumn remained green. There was no spectacle of changing leaf colour, no arrival of the daffodils and bluebells. The settlers set about changing that as soon as they had time to plant the bulbs, the poplars, and other deciduous trees which have become a feature of the southern and central landscapes, their April colour creating a dramatic touch in the dry high country of the centre of both Islands, the plains of Hawke's Bay and inland Marlborough. But in the north, with its sub-tropical climate, many of the hardy plants of the northern hemisphere did not establish so happily, nor did they colour in autumn, and when they became available the tender plants which were more suited to the warm environment were grown instead. Before long some of these were to become wayside weeds: bulbs from South Africa, the heavy scented datura, the ginger, the lantana, and the arum and belladonna lilies.

In the north the summers lasted longer, the spring flowers came in winter. Throughout the country the sunlight was brighter, the skies bluer, the atmosphere so clear that visibility was 80 to 160 kilometres on fine days, until it became clouded by smoke which hung in the air for months at a time as forest fires raged. The Canterbury Plains, the size of Holland, had scarcely any natural trees, being largely scrub and tussock. Lord Lyttelton, after whom Lyttelton Harbour, the Port of Christchurch was named, used to watch it from the garden of Mt. Peel on the foothills of the Southern Alps, and saw "small gigs and drays slowly moving across the plain from all points of the compass."[2]

The tussock of South Canterbury had not been cleared when, the *Lancashire Witch,* arrived at Timaru with settlers in 1863, and "when they saw the tall waving tussock which then covered the downs above the cliffs they were delighted, thinking they had arrived in time to help with the harvest."[3] It was not many years, however, before these fertile plains were planted with crops and fruit and gardens, and landmarks were made by the trees of parks and farm shelterbelts.

Although it is generally temperate the weather can exasperate the gardener by its frequent changes, particularly in the warmer months of the year. Temperatures fluctuate almost from day to day, but do not affect the growth of a great range of plants originating from different zones of the world which now grow together.

While some domesticated plants have run wild to the extent of being declared noxious weeds like the blackberry, (introduced by the first missionaries), others have been deliberately spread by well-meaning gardeners. In Otago, for example, there are the Russell lupins, a strain of fine colours which have become a tourist attraction around the great southern lakes on the road to Milford Sound, and at Mt. Cook. So absurdly out of place are they among the alpine vegetation, that the contrast they provide against the tawny, wild land of this high altitude provides a bright note of surprise.

The smallest of New Zealand's three main islands is Stewart Island, which, for all its southernmost situation, has a mild, even climate with temperatures that seldom drop to freezing point yet never rise above the pleasantly warm. It is a rugged, bushclad place with tall granite peaks, deep inlets, and unspoilt bays. The few gardens of note can boast flowers all year round and of some tender kinds that could not be considered on the nearby mainland. They are superbly sheltered by the surrounding bush, with views and quietude that could amount to a gardener's paradise.

Southland is only about 30 kilometres across the Foveaux Strait, but this beautiful farming province has cold winters, bleak and wet

1. Hedychium *or common ginger grows wild in Auckland and Northland adding a most attractive dash of colour to the roadside.*

2. *Eden Garden is built on the site of an old quarry on the slopes of an extinct volcano in the heart of suburban Auckland. The micro-climate provided by its various aspects enables plants from the cold hardy to sub-tropical, and even tropical, to be grown. It contains species that grow throughout the North Island, from north to south and all the intermediate humid to cool or rain-drenched areas between – a botanic garden representative in a small area of New Zealand's contrasting climates.*

Opposite page. *Northland is the warmest and most humid part of the country, ideal for sub-tropical plants. This old church at Russell is enlivened by the modern hibiscus in its grounds.*

on the average, spring delaying its appearance till the very last. But the hardy bulbs from the northern hemisphere, familiar spring flowers, make no fleeting gesture for they thrive in the rich plains and valleys. This part of the country has the same horticultural potential as Holland and among the more recent settlers has attracted Dutchmen who grow tulips in their traditional way, so adding bands of brilliant colour among the grasslands of the sheep and cattle stations.

Queenstown and the surrounding areas, with a short, bright summer and wonderful long daylight evenings, has some lovely home gardens. In the public Government Gardens, the sequoia or Big Tree of California, has reached giant proportions to set off the grandeur of the mountain scenery. In autumn, the colours of the trees attracts and amazes especially in the areas frequently visited by tourists such as the old goldmine village of Arrowtown.

In these colder parts of the country the hardy northern hemisphere conifers like the larch and the Oregon Pine have adapted well to the more austere climate.

Had farmers not planted deciduous trees, some parts of the South Island would be stark indeed. Central Otago, with the lowest rainfall in the country, has a climate continental in contrast with its neighbouring Southland and the southern west coast, yet the apricot trees for which it is famous become a sheet of pink blossom in spring and the leaves turn gold and crimson in autumn. Golden fruit, the golden poplars in autumn, and the same burnished colour in the grass tinges the countryside, but very little remains of the mineral gold which attracted the early adventurers to this high, dry country.

The particular character of gardens in each region is influenced not only by climate but by historical background. Organised settlement did not start until 1840, and whether by design or coincidence the areas chosen for the different groups of people were often similar in climate to the places from which they originated. This was particularly the case in the South Island. Once the settlers had time to plant trees, it was natural that they should choose those with which they were most familiar, and they were to find that some species grew faster than in their native lands.

Eighty French settlers arrived at Akaroa on Banks Peninsula in 1840, and this is one place that has secured an atmosphere found in few other parts, for an attempt has been made to retain the image of the past — the French street and place names, picturesque old cottages and quaint churches.

Grapes and walnuts, pepper trees and palms, are plants that survive from those early days. Akaroa's pleasant, frost-free climate encourages adventurous gardening and is in direct contrast to the extremes of the Canterbury Plains which lie over the Port Hills to the west, but in this it could be regarded as typical of many other coastal areas. Opposite, on the West Coast of the South Island, Karamea boasts of its 'winterless' climate, too.

Kapiti Island, 48 kilometres from Wellington on the west coast, also has a micro-climate, like Stewart Island, although the mainland coast is unusually warm. The headquarters of whalers in the early days, credit is given them for the introduction of some of the sub-tropical plants which grow so well in this area. Kapiti Island became the centre of operations of the Maori chief Te Rauparaha, who raided and plundered the tribes on the west coasts of both Islands and the pakeha in their settlements. After Te Rauparaha's capture, Kapiti became a Maori-owned farm with Phoenix date palm trees at the entrance to the home. The home burned down, little but the palms remaining. Today all but a small northern portion has become a bird sanctuary, the only garden on the now bushclad island being that tended by the ranger's wife. This historic island lends its name to the beautiful Kapiti Coast area which it shelters, with several growing towns and settlements, a mild climate where gardens thrive and beautiful beaches and bushclad hills to make it one of the outstanding residential areas in the Wellington region.

Further up the coast is a fast-developing horticultural area in the Horowhenua and Manawatu where large areas of vegetables and farmland are now being redeveloped into smaller allotments with a great diversity of crops, especially flowers and fruit.

Opposite page. *Deciduous trees were among the first plants introduced to New Zealand, for in a land of evergreens, they were (and still are) a nostalgic reminder of home. Burnished gold graces the countryside in many parts in autumn, the most colourful being the poplars of shelterbelts and riverbanks from Wanganui and Hawke's Bay southwards, but the Botanic Gardens in Christchurch must surely be the most celebrated and the most photographed.*

2. *Hardy heaths and ox-eye daisies near Mt. Ruapehu provide a colourful contrast against the dry browns of sun-burned tussock and the hazy greys of distant peaks.*

3. *Old roses planted by the French settlers in Akaroa still grow beside the town's cottages which, along with the street names and mild climate, all contribute to the French character and atmosphere.*

Many of the islands in the Hauraki Gulf or round the coast of the Auckland peninsula are of volcanic origin. Some are suitable for gardens, like the populated and pleasant Waiheke Island from which people commute by ferry to work in the city, but perhaps the most famous island is Kawau, which Sir George Grey, once the Governor of New Zealand, bought in 1862 and to which he eventually retired. A keen and knowledgeable naturalist, he spent 26 years of his life and fortune making a home and garden on the large island, creating his idea of a little paradise. He bought plants from Auckland nurserymen and imported many exotic sub-tropical trees, fruits and flowering shrubs. They even included Brazilian coconuts and other palms which he hoped would provide food for the monkeys he set free, along with wallabies, deer, opossums, peacocks and kookaburras.

In those days there were no restrictions on what could be brought into the country, and as the plants ran wild so did many of the animals, with disastrous damage to the natural flora. Even the monkeys on Kawau had to be shot because they increased too well, but the wallabies and opossums continue to occupy the bush. At least Grey's introductions were confined by the sea to his island home, for their colonisation was detrimental to the vegetation and nothing remains of the original plants except mature pine trees, the palms, and a few others. Now the Lands and Survey Department with the Hauraki Gulf Maritime Park Board which administers the property, has made an effort to revive Grey's garden around the recently restored Mansion House, his old home, utilising as far as research can reveal, the same varieties of plants which grew there. The island today is a popular tourist, yachting and pleasure resort.

Gardens that leave an indelible impression are those set amid the steam of the thermal volcanic region around Rotorua. This natural resource of boiling pools and steam, once used by the Maori for cooking purposes, is now used for heating glasshouses to produce tomatoes, mushrooms and for propagating plants and tropical flowers. Home gardeners also make use of this valuable commodity.

Sir George Grey, an early Governor of New Zealand made Kawau Island in the Hauraki Gulf a little paradise, importing exotic flora and fauna to create his ideal garden. Today it is a popular tourist attraction administered by the Hauraki Gulf Maritime Park Board. Kawau Island has some magnificent specimen trees, oaks growing beside Moreton Bay figs and phoenix palms lining the entranceway. Date palms were also frequently planted in those days, grown from seed. The only recorded pair which set fruit, grew out of the top of a nurseryman's abandoned glasshouse in Auckland.

2

The lakes in the central North Island range from the inland sea of Lake Taupo to the many beautiful smaller lakes in the Rotorua area, set about with beautiful gardens and homes that meet the water's edge. The damp humid climate here is in direct contrast to the deep, cold fiord-like lakes of the far south or the glacial lakes of the central South Island. Here the gardens surrounding the high country sheep stations are generally sparse because of the very short growing season but some success has been achieved in the past. At Godley Peaks homestead at Tekapo, Canadian sugar maples were planted to line the drive, peonies were grown beside the house along with roses and some native plants of the region, especially the giant *Ranunculus lyallii*.

In Auckland, Northland, the Bay of Plenty and Gisborne – the warmest parts of the country, hibiscus and many other tender flowers, lemons and other exotic fruits can be seen ripening in most gardens year-round. In the less densely populated areas of these regions, tropical fruiting trees are gradually changing the typical country scene, with orchards of citrus, tamarillos (or tree tomatoes) from the South American highlands, the babaco, a half-hardy hybrid paw paw, and the pepino, a small bush-fruit. There are rows of macadamias, a delicious hard-skinned nut from Queensland, the avocado from Central America, and leading the parade, *Actinidis chinensis* from China, which has been given the New Zealand name 'kiwifruit' because it is grown so widely and is such a profitable fruit for overseas markets.

Kiwifruit is also changing the country scene in Nelson, another area with a warm micro-climate where apples, hops and tobacco have long been major horticultural industries. Now kiwifruit has largely displaced tobacco.

The Bay of Plenty, where citrus fruits once grew exclusively, has a flower festival every year when one of the prettiest girls is chosen as citrus queen, but lemon and orange plantations are gradually being phased out before the rows of kiwifruit.

This beautiful sub-tropical region was a great food-growing area before the arrival of Europeans, with kumara and taro the staple crop. The skill of the Maori as gardeners was noticed by Colenso

3

Opposite page. *The tranquil setting of a home by the water's edge. Several exotic trees have been planted for effect and they contrast splendidly with the dark, rounded forms of the native species in the background.*

2. *A citrus orchard near Kerikeri, an area which has become renowned for its produce. Exotic fruiting trees are gradually changing the typical country scene in many of the warmer parts of the land, especially in the sparsely populated regions of Northland, the Bay of Plenty and Nelson.*

3. *A curious contrast at Motueka, Nelson, where a bed of lilies grows in a garden next to a tobacco farm. The expanding kiwifruit industry is largely responsible for the decline in tobacco cropping in this sunny micro-climate.*

2

on his first journey to the East Cape. He commented, "These plantations were large, in nice condition, and looked very neat, the plants being planted in true quincunx order, and the ground strewed with fine white sand, with which the large pendulous and dark green shield-like leaves of the plants beautifully contrasted; some of the leaves measuring more than 2 feet in length – the blade only. Small screens formed of the young branches of *Leptospermum scoparium* (manuka) to shelter the young plants from the violence of the winds, intercepted the ground in every direction."

Gisborne, the servicing centre of the East Cape, is warm and humid, and has many exotic flowers and fruits in the gardens. It was the first place to successfully grow avocados, long before their commercial potential was realised.

It is impossible to describe the great variation in climate in each region and the specialties grown in the districts within these, but Taranaki with its snow-capped Mt. Egmont stands out because so many plants from all over the world grow in the lovely gardens, spring being the most colourful time. In the rich volcanic soil everything grows so well that it has become the most important centre of ornamental plant production in New Zealand.

Because certain plants grow better on one coast than another, thrive in the south better than those in the north, or more luxuriantly on the humid coast or the mountain slopes, does not mean that the modern gardener takes the easy course and grows what naturally does best in his particular climate and soil. Like the early settlers, he usually tries to grow some plants to which he has a sentimental attachment, defying nature, but because of the tolerance of the climate finds he can manipulate it at times to satisfy himself. If he neglects his garden, weeds take over swiftly, and given time, nearby bush could within a few years cause it to revert to the wild state. But on established grasslands the forest would be unlikely to return.

On the whole, this land of contrasts is a happy place for those who would make gardens, large or small, about their homes and towns, providing in one area or another the conditions required for almost every plant they could desire to grow.

Opposite page. In the natural bush on the lower slopes of Mt Egmont, the tolerance of the climate allows giant rhododendrons to thrive in an area of land owned by the Pukeiti Rhododendron Trust.

2. Pukekura Park, close to the city of New Plymouth, is an attractive garden with colourful sub-tropical plants mingling with native trees and ferns. The main feature is a lake in the centre of the gardens, with a kiosk and an enchanting view of Mount Egmont as a backdrop. There is an orchid and begonia house, and rhododendrons grow especially well. It is a place worth visiting at any time of year.

1. W.C. Davies, Banks Lecture to the R.N.Z. Institute of Horticulture, 1949.

2, 3. *South Canterbury, A Record of Settlement.* A. Gillespie, South Canterbury Centennial Committee, 1958.

old farm gardens

Throughout New Zealand's gardening history, there has been a marked tendency towards the recreation of the English garden. In the case of the large farms and sheep stations, the urge was to reproduce either the type of garden associated with the stately homes, which were landscaped with large trees, sweeping lawns, and artificially created lakes and ponds, or the more formal design of the Victorian gardens, where flowers were enclosed with borders of shrubby 'box' or lavender. Some of the old homesteads which remain to this day have gardens which are typically English, yet time has blended them into their background until they have become traditionally New Zealand.

The early runholders for all their determination could not change the rugged new land, primitive and mountainous, into the gentle, time-worn, undulating countryside they remembered, nor could they replace the remaining natural forest or bush with their beloved woodlands. But there were successful attempts.

At Mt. Peel the homestead of the pioneer Acland family, there is a plantation of established oaks, beeches, and pines through which a path winds from the century-old, red brick house to the little family church made of river stones. In spring the wood is gay with bluebells and primroses, later with rhododendrons, and in December there is the extraordinary sight of thousands of giant Himalayan lilies, *Cardiocrinum giganteum,* on two to three metre stems, their sweet scent heavy on the air.

The bulbs were thought to have been planted by one of the first gardeners employed by J.B.A. Acland, a certain W.W. Smith, who later became superintendent of such public gardens as Ashburton Domain and Pukekura Park and was an early advocate of the use of native plants for gardens. He trained at several stately homes in England before coming to Mt. Peel in the 1870s as a knowledgeable landscape gardener. He was thought also to have planted the rhododendrons and some of the other flowering plants which have naturalised throughout the woodland and added greatly to its charm.

But this is not the only garden at an old station homestead where the lily has naturalised so luxuriantly. It has done so at 'Westoe', near Marton in the North Island, in large gardens in Hawke's Bay, and also at 'Coldstream', near Ashburton in South Canterbury, and other parts of the country.

Not far from Mt. Peel at Peel Forest there is another interesting station homestead, which dates back to 1855 and has been devotedly preserved and restored by the owners, where the fascinating lilies have also naturalised under the trees.

This farm was pioneered by Francis Jollie who arrived in Nelson in 1842 and built a large home where he established a fine garden. When he came to Peel Forest he planted deciduous trees around the house and made a garden, most of which has been preserved by his descendants. He was a friend of Edgar Stead, the ornithologist, who was to become famous for his rhododendron hybrids. His daughter, Mrs D.H.S. Martin, recalls that he once exchanged a bush canary's egg for some rhododendron seedlings and cuttings. He lined his driveway with Douglas firs, which he imported growing in their own soil in Wardian cases; no seed had been germinated from earlier shipments. In 1859 his neighbour, J.B.A. Acland received a consignment of plants from Veitch and Son, the famous Exeter nurserymen who distributed many fine trees and shrubs around the world. Included in this shipment were five small sequoias in pots; probably the first of this species to be introduced into New Zealand. A magnificent sequoia stands before the Acland homestead today. In many other gardens this tree was also given pride of place and they tower today over 30 metres high.

2

3

Opposite page. *A one-hectare lake is a dramatic feature of the garden at 'Centrewood', Waimate. In spring, bright rhododendrons and massed azaleas reflect in the water. White swans, introduced to further the illusion of an English setting, are still comparatively uncommon in New Zealand.*

2. *In 1861 C.G. Tripp and J.B.A. Acland dissolved their partnership and divided their South Canterbury leaseholds. Acland opted for Mount Peel which his descendants have occupied ever since. A feature of this historic place are the fine specimen trees – oak, elm, beech and a magnificent sequoia – all especially imported by J.B.A. Acland over 100 years ago.*

3. *The old family church of the Mount Peel homestead complements its woodland setting.*

The giant Himalayan lily, Cardiocrinum giganteum *was one of the bulbs which naturalised and now flowers in thousands under the old oaks and beeches of the woodland established between the homestead and the old family church, Mount Peel. The drooping, funnel-shaped flowers of this shade-loving plant are borne on stems that can attain a height of three metres.*

Opposite page. *The small-leaved* Buxus, *commonly called box, was frequently used to edge the formal gardens of the late nineteenth century. The original hedges have been retained at places such as 'Centrewood' (pictured) and 'Orari Gorge' in the South Island, and 'Westoe' in the North Island; occasionally one also finds them still in botanical gardens.*

2

For as well as the symbols of Home – the oak, the elm and the beech – the exotic species which were spreading into the English garden were also planted by settlers establishing gardens in New Zealand – magnolias and rhododendrons from India and Asia, camellias from China and Japan, Californian redwood, the Umbrella pine from Australia, the curious Monkey Puzzle tree from Chile, the Monterey cypress, *Cupressus macrocarpa,* and eucalyptus from Australia. The best of those that remain in the New Zealand countryside today are classed as of historical importance in official records and hopefully preserved from destruction.

Another historic farmstead where these earlier trees are still to be found is Orari Gorge, South Canterbury, neighbouring the Mt. Peel Station. It was owned by Acland's partner, C.G. Tripp, who was also keenly interested in creating a fine garden. He imported in tiny pots from Australia what became a eucalyptus plantation and other special features of the present garden – the magnificent copper beech, the oaks, cedars, and larches.

3

The first people to establish large sheep stations started their new lives far from their fellow man, living in humble huts made from logs or earthen sods, tree fern poles and totara bark, and it is recorded that even these dwellings were occasionally surrounded by small, nostalgic gardens containing vegetables, annuals and roses.

Considering that the settlers' only means of breaking in the land was by bullock team and horse and plough, the pioneering years seem , in retrospect, very short. Most of the stalwart pioneers took up their land titles or leases around the 1850s and were largely responsible for the destruction of the primeval forests in the north and the great tussock lands in the south. The speed with which they reduced the great wilderness to bare virgin soil and succeeded in establishing the sweeter grasses and clovers to support their flocks of sheep was incredibly swift.

It seems amazing that the settlers were so blind to the beauty and character of the native vegetation and yet loved trees so well, for these were the first things they planted to relieve the monotony of the barren countryside they had created by fire and axe.

Opposite page. Francis Jollie lined his driveway with deciduous trees, oaks and elms, and Douglas firs which he imported in Wardian cases. They create a woodland effect as one drives up to the house, with bluebells and primroses lining the verge in spring.

2. Jollie's old homestead at Peel Forest estate with the front partially covered with Banksia roses and the garden still displaying many old roses and shrubs planted by him. The homestead dates back to 1855 and has been devotedly maintained and restored by the present owners.

3. The Banksia rose, Rosa banksia *'Lutea', named for Sir Joseph Banks who accompanied Cook on the expedition of the* Endeavour, *was a favourite rose of the early missionaries and settlers in the far north and Akaroa. It is still popular with gardeners today.*

'Orari Gorge' was founded by C.G. Tripp, a neighbour and partner of J.B.A. Acland of Mount Peel. They were both interested in trees and making a garden and imported many of the present magnificent trees which remain a notable feature of the station.

1. The magnificent copper beech which stands in front of the house was imported along with several oaks, elms and euclypts, by C.G. Tripp in the 1870s.

2. The vegetable garden with its neat borders of box. The whole garden is tended today by one man, whereas in old times without modern implements and knowledge it would have taken many more to maintain it.

3. A herb garden at 'Orari' revived to meet a present-day interest in these plants which were much used in earlier times.

Opposite page. An interesting background picture of the old homestead at 'Orari Gorge' which gives a indication of the size of home and garden typical of large farms in the early days.

2

Opposite page. *The common woodland bluebell is widely cultivated for its lilac-blue bell-shaped flowers. It is easily grown in most soils, naturalising freely in grassy areas, woodland or lightly shaded conditions. Bluebells were one of the bulbs that reminded people of home and inevitably they were planted in similar settings.*

2. *Box hedges like these at 'Orari Gorge' were fashionable at the time these gardens were made and are still retained in some of them.*

3. *'Orari Gorge'. A general view of the ornamental garden backed by the original eucalypts planted by C.G. Tripp a hundred years ago.*

3

2

The impassable swamps, the dense raupo and flax and tangled scrub in Canterbury required more than usual pioneering skills. John Grigg who founded 'Longbeach', spent a lifetime transforming a great swamp between the Ashburton River and Hinds into one of the finest farms in the South Island. He undertoook the colossal task of draining 13,000 hectares in 1864 and by 1871 he had built the first homestead. Around it he created a garden 16 hectares in extent, featuring glorious old trees, wide lawns and a lake stocked with goldfish and carp. The basic plan was John Grigg's, and the gardens with their natural planting of rhododendrons and liliums reflect the ideals and vision of this pioneer.

The lakes on these estates were created for pleasure and landscape effect just as they were in the English gardens and cannot be compared to the dams or large ponds which are made to conserve water on today's farms. They are found repeatedly on estates where the home and garden were built about 100 years ago.

For about twenty years the great effort of clearing and cultivating, removing the stumps of burnt trees, went on, but by the 1870s the runholders had achieved their main objectives and were able to think of providing finer things for their families. By then they were well enough off to start building substantial dwellings of pitsawn timber, selected from heart kauri, totara, and other solid native trees that proved far more durable than the English oak. They also used bricks manufactured on the site. These materials have enabled some houses to endure to this day, but many of the finest wooden houses of the pioneers have been destroyed by fires.

With the establishment of permanent homes and the approach of more prosperous times, the age of gardening for pleasure began. Most of the early sheep station owners came from cultured backgrounds where gardens were part of their heritage and a home was not considered complete without grand and restful surroundings. So they made wide sweeping drives to take their fine horses and carriages, sometimes lining them with avenues of

planes and elms, cedars or pines, and they laid extensive lawns on which they planted shade trees. Under the trees they planted bluebells, primroses, and sweet violets, and these gradually naturalised and spread. They made formal flower beds of the annuals and perennials they loved, the marigolds and granny's bonnets, shrub roses, lavender, and lily of the valley. And they trained rambling roses and blue wisteria up the verandah posts of their houses, where the same plants can be seen today, the names of the roses long forgotten.

Some of the homesteads now owned by the Historic Places Trust have maintained 'old world' gardens around them with emphasis on the first hardy ornamentals to be grown.

At 'Coldstream' in Ashburton, not far from Longbeach, John Studholme made a feature of two lakes in front of his charming home which was erected in 1870. The lakes were scooped out by the efforts of men and horses, and were fed from a stream about 45 metres distant which meandered through flax, raupo, and cabbage trees. Nearby he planted rhododendrons, blue-gums, pines and black poplars now gigantic and a hundred years old, and an orchard. By 1937 all the fruit trees, save one huge old pear, had died, and the original orchard was high in cocksfoot and overgrown with periwinkle escaped from the shrubberies. This area was cleared and planted in English oaks.

Opposite page. *A glimpse of the courtyard at 'Coldstream' through a brick archway.*

2. *At 'Coldstream', Ashburton, John Studholme made two lakes as a feature of his garden and a viewpoint in front of the long house above it. Mrs D. Studholme's account of the garden describes it as a perfect example of an English landscaped garden. In spring, rhododendrons and azaleas are a striking element of this old farm garden.*

1. The Chatham Island forget-me-not, Myosotidium hortensis, *is also an excellent feature plant when grown close to water. It is still popular with home gardeners but not easy to grow away from its nature shores.*

2. *Hostas are favourite plants in moist garden situations as at 'Titoki Point' and 'Coldstream'. Their large, oval-pointed, ribbed leaves create an interesting and decorative texture when planted by water or shaded foreground situations.*

3. *Rhododendrons were popular introductions in the early days of settlement.*

In 1956 when the owner decided to redevelop the garden, the stage was already set. Rhododendrons went under the oaks, with the little, wild, woodland cyclamen near their trunks. Quantities of primulas were planted round the ponds with other damp or shade-loving specimens, such as hostas, trilliums, rodgersia, *Lobelia cardinalis,* arums, acanthus, ferns, hypericum and astilbes. Chatham Island forget-me-nots were found to grow excellently beside the rhododendrons, azaleas on sunny banks where they could reflect in the pond, and cherries and magnolias on the large expanse of lawn. And when one wing of the sprawling, cold, uncomfortable second house was removed about this time, the large rough concrete foundation blocks were used to construct a curved wall down the terrace, on top of which now grow brooms, forsythia, senecios, and cistus. The happiest part of the garden is undoubtedly the area of the original planting – the *Magnolia grandiflora* and the huge camellia bushes with flowers of pale pink, darker pink, striped pink and white, rising from a sea of bluebells to over 5.4 metres high, protected from the wind and frost by the hazel nut walk.[1]

Thus the English way of life became traditional also in New Zealand, particularly in the South Island where it is reflected in these old and established homes and gardens. The climate favoured the planting of all the hardy trees, shrubs, perennials, and bulbs which grew in the British Isles, and hardy northern hemisphere plants are still the basis of gardening in the south.

South Canterbury abounds in the romance of the early pioneering days. A magnificent estate that has remained in the family for several generations is at Rakaia where grain is a golden product of the plains with their hot, dry summers. 'Holmeslea' always had a lovely garden, and many of the original features have been maintained. The owners landscaping the grounds and using Mr Holmes scientific knowledge of plant breeding, have raised their own distinct hybrid and seedling rhododendrons and liliums to add special interest. Farmers throughout the country now take more pride in the immediate surroundings of their homes. Many of them are diverting their land into horticultural crops for export instead of the traditional livestock, and those with knowledge of flower growing are finding this aspect also has commercial prospects.

It is exciting in a land only forming its traditions to discover that descendants of the first pioneers, particularly those who founded the larger farms and sheep stations which have been the backbone of our farming industry, are still living in the original farm houses, some restored, others added to or modernised, and yet others replaced and gardens maintained. It is encouraging to find other current owners caring for the properties with an equal respect for their historical significance.

4. *'Holmeslea' at Rakaia is in the drier region where grains are the main agricultural product. This old home is surrounded by a garden in which the owners take a great personal interest and rhododendrons and liliums are a specialty. The farm has been in family hands for several generations. 'Holmeslea' always had a lovely garden and many of the original features have been lovingly maintained, even to a century-old wisteria which encircles the balconied house.*

4

Another historic home which is in good hands was built by Sir William Fox, one of the more colourful of the early politicians, who in 1860 purchased for sheep farming a large block of land in the Rangitikei district, in the lower half of the North Island. In 1874 he built a fine, solid, two-storied house with a tower and named it 'Westoe'. He laid the foundations for the garden as it stands today, a sweeping drive lined with trees and lawns on which he planted copper beech, cedar of Lebanon and *Pinus patula,* giants today, where he entertained at colourful garden parties.

The estate was purchased in 1885 by the Howard family, who still take special pride in the beautiful stand of native bush (which includes a 1000 year old kahikatea), as well as the arboretum of trees which displays glorious autumn colour in the deciduous species, groves of rhododendrons and magnolias, some outstanding metasequoia or dawn redwoods, gingkos or maidenhair trees, and gigantic Californian redwoods. The Howard's own contribution is a delightful, eight-hectare park and garden.[2]

Some of the pine shelterbelts planted by Sir William Fox still stand. The lower half of the North Island was clad in heavy forest until the settlers came, and when the land was cleared they felt the full force of the winds that swept across their farms and gardens. Native trees grew slowly, so for quick shelter they turned to faster growing conifers. The Californian *Pinus radiata,* first used as an ornamental in gardens, became the accepted tree for this purpose in most parts of the country. It was not until 1900 that its economic potential was realised, with the result that it now occupies great areas of land once covered by native forests, mountain tussock and sand dunes.

Some of the finest and most interesting gardens are around the homesteads of large farms in the central parts of the North Island, in high altitudes where alpine plants and deciduous trees grow to perfection. In autumn they complement the dark greens of bush-clad slopes and emerald green fields, but usually hidden behind sheltering belts of pine. Several farmers who have been there since the land was first cleared have created interesting large gardens about their homesteads. Mr and Mrs Ian Gordon of Utiku have an extensive collection of rare and beautiful conifers and a lake below the home guarded zealously by two white swans. Peacocks were introduced and have taken to the wild.

Another plantsman farmer of the same area, R.J. Berry of Abbotsford Station, Tiniroto, compiled a complete catalogue of his neighbour's trees for the Trust in 1982. He also has a notable collection of his own trees planted in the same concept. Both these farms are in rigorous hilly conditions, where the climate is mild but drought is not uncommon, and the trees have been well tested for the qualities necessary for survival.

A well-known former politician and farmer, Ormond Wilson gave his Sanson farm homestead and garden to the Crown as a public reserve. It is a tranquil place with a natural landscape of native trees with some fine deciduous species that colour well in autumn. It also has *Lilium giganteum* naturalised under trees and the place is most visited when the daffodils cover the fields around the house in spring.

Shelterbelts are characteristic of farm and large gardens. They form an interesting backdrop, especially when they are a mixture of evergreen and deciduous trees, which colour well inland.

One farmer in Gisborne was determined to gather together on his estate all the worthwhile trees and shrubs suitable for cultivation in New Zealand.

On his sheep station at 'Eastwoodhill', D.W. Cook started a garden and arboretum importing thousands of plants of horticultural worth which were rare or unknown in New Zealand. His idea was to procure these trees for the future farmers and gardeners of New Zealand before they were unobtainable or became prohibited imports.

Many of Cook's importations, rarities that he propagated and dispersed around the country, are now treasured in other gardens, but he is equally well remembered for his part in visualising the Pukeiti Rhododendron Trust in Taranaki, of which he was one of the founders.

2

3

Opposite page. *'Westoe', the historic home of politician Sir James Fox, overlooks the Rangitikei River eight kilometres from Marton. Built in 1874, it is still surrounded by the original garden which has been faithfully preserved and added to by the present owners, and is notable for its arboretum of rare and beautiful old trees.*

2. *A neighbour of Douglas Cook of 'Eastwoodhill' was R.J. Berry who also created an arboretum on his sheep station at Tiniroto.*

3. *Daffodils naturalised on a grassy hillside at Waikanae where the Field family established the first farm.*

54

Opposite page. *The arboretum at 'Eastwoodhill' with some of the fine old trees prominent against the seasonal dry grass of a hot Gisborne summer.*

A tranquil portion of the garden of Mr and Mrs Ian Gordon at Utiku in the central North Island.

When he became too old to manage the property, he sold it to H.B. Williams of Turihaua Station near Gisborne, who, recognising the national value of the arboretum, gifted the property, on Mr. Cook's death in 1975, to the specially created 'Eastwoodhill Trust Board' to ensure that the arboretum would be preserved for posterity.

Gordon Collier, a sheep farmer who is a trained horticulturist, has one of the most extensive gardens around his homestead, 'Titoki Point' at Rangiwaea where giant redwoods planted by his parents in 1923 now provide shelter for a steep valley which he has landscaped in a circular terraced design with cascading water and pools falling to a fascinating bog garden and woodland garden. It is ideal for hardy plants and alpines and in spring is a glorious sight with rhododendrons, bulbs and a fascinating collection of perennials, covering many years of collecting rare and unusual plants. In autumn the colours of deciduous trees stand out against the dark green of the redwoods. He has extended the garden with a 3 hectare arboretum of rare of unusual conifers, and on the hills surrounding the home is developing 15 hectares of parkland on those parts of the farm within view of the garden, where sheep will graze in an romantic setting. He was greatly influenced by the English landscaped gardens after visits there and in the modern concept is carrying on the traditions of the early settler who made large gardens on their estates.

Few women gardened in a serious way in the early days. Their household, family, and social responsibilities seldom allowed time for such pursuits, although they no doubt enjoyed the more leisurely tasks associated with gardening; the men were the plant connoisseurs and garden planners. But modern improvements in the home and a changing outloook on women's status offered greater opportunities for freedom of action and encourage women to become actively interested,, Among early women pioneers noted for their gardening ability was the mother of A. P. Howard of 'Westoe', who imported trees and other exotic material from overseas and took a practical interest in developing this outstanding garden. Her interest in plants has been handed down for three generations of the family, and in 'Blue Cliffs Station' homestead, South Canterbury, another woman, Miss Paulette Woodhouse is also "the modern gardener representing the third generation of her family to care for the garden." Miss Woodhouse

is able to care for the garden almost single-handed by using some methods which may interest others with extensive gardens. She uses sheep to graze the green expanse (down to the Otaio Valley) with a light electric fence to keep them enclosed. Sheep will eat bluebells and primroses, but if they are kept at low stocking rate will not hurt rhododendrons, daffodils, colchicums and snow-drops.

The area under the trees is a beautiful patchwork of bluebells with a variety of other spring bulbs including fritillarias. This will be mown at Christmas. Further on is an area with later flowering woodlanders, aquilegias, lilies, monkshood and thalictrum, this mown in autumn. A small patch lying to the sun, a blaze of colour in the early spring, will be sprayed with Paraquat in early April. These methods make it possible to tend the large areas and to have the effect of a woodland garden without allowing the grasses and weeds to get the upper hand. [3]

'Titoki Point' near Taihape in the central North Island, has an interesting valley garden with many unusual trees, a fascinating rock garden and a bog area with pools and cascades. It is made accessible by a series of small terraces with descending steps edged by weeping Japanese maples. Ten hectares of the farm is also landscaped with trees under which the sheep graze, following the ideals of the English landscaped estate.

Opposite page. *The water and bog garden is a spectacular sight in spring with rhododendrons, primulas and many other interesting plants in flower.*

2. *A glimpse of the valley garden*

3. *A part of the valley garden which has been terraced and planted with a fascinating collection of perennials. The steps are bordered with red weeping maples, which along with the other deciduous trees create a most colourful spectacle in autumn.*

Mrs W.P. Hayes beautiful home at 'Centrewood', Waimate, was built from bricks made on the site and pit-sawn timbers from the great totara forests which once covered the area. The Hayes family millled the trees and later farmed an area around where the house stands. It was planned by a French architect, Maurice de H'Arveau Duval, an imaginative design unusual for the era, at least in New Zealand. It has a French elegance and style which is complemented by the design of the garden, with its huge old trees, many of them choice and unusual, often collected on journeys overseas by Mrs. Winifred Hayes, whose abiding passion is the care and maintenance of her garden. Still taking an active interest in the place, she has seen her plantings of mollis azaleas mature around the man-made lake with its white swans, glorious sweeps of liliums and peonies among the flowering plants, roses and magnolias, and her own hybrids of her favourite plants, especially rhododendrons.

There are several notable gardens in this area made by women. Not all are of the traditional kind with wooded dells, bluebells, shrubs and beds of roses. Mrs W.L. Doyle whose family were pioneers at Ruapuna has created a cottage garden and large rock gardens after the fashion of Gertrude Jekyll, a famous English landscape designer and advocate of the cottage garden. The rock and alpine garden cult educated by the alpine plant authority and explorer Reginald Farrer also found a following in New Zealand early this century, and both of these people would have been pleased with Mrs. Doyle's garden. Her large rock gardens contain a collection of the rarest and loveliest of alpine plants which thrive in this cold area where snow lies heavily in winter. Shelterbelts protect the large garden with its drifts of rhododendrons, peonies and other hardy perennials.

One of the notable gardens in the North Island is that of 'The Ridges', near Rata. This was created largely by the efforts of Mrs M. V. Marshall, who in 1924 came as a bride to the old station, which dated back to 1863. She found only shelterbelts, some unusual conifers, and a 30-metre, columnar golden *Chamaecyparis* towering beside the house. Since then she has planted a great range of cold climate plants which in this area, cold and wet in winter, grow to perfection. Massive drifts and groups of one genus – mature magnolias, camellias, rhododendrons and azaleas – makes the garden quite breathtaking in spring, as it is in autumn when the cold air brings colour to the deciduous trees.

The long drive is planted with large rhododendrons and terminates with Young's weeping birch, a rare form of the silver birch. Underplantings of small shrubs, lilies, and other bulbs create interest all the year round. The garden spills over into the fields, where daffodils and bluebells are naturalised, and extends to the frontage on the main highway where a large area has been planted in mixed exotic trees.

Now the 60 year old homestead is set within the one and a half hectares of garden, personally supervised and planted by Mrs Marshall over the years, sheltered from behind by a magnificent stand of kahikatea, and with a panoramic view opening out before it.

Most of the large sheep runs were so isolated that they were able to choose the best site for their homesteads, whereas the smaller farms which came later were almost invariably situated as close to the roads and the milking sheds as possible, encouraging little incentive to landscaping as the owners became more prosperous.

It is a good sign that these old gardens are still being cared for, their old trees maturing gracefully and maintained with a fraction of the labour required in the early days. It augurs well for their continuing existence, remaining little changed for future generations to look back upon.

Opposite page. *Mrs Winifred Hayes of 'Centrewood' with a Macabeanum hybrid rhododendron 'Joybells', raised by herself and acknowledged as an outstanding new variety.*

2. *Mrs Doyle's garden at Ruapuna in South Canterbury has a notable collection of alpine plants which lie under a blanket of snow in winter. This interesting place was carved from grassland and tall shelter was necessary before establishing a garden. The stones were carried from the fields to make the garden walls.*

3. *Rhododendrons at 'The Ridges', Marton. Along with other cold climate shrubs and flowers, these ever popular exotics are planted in drifts which produce a strong and vivid impact in their seasons.*

1. From an account by Mrs Derek Studholme sent to the author in 1972. 'Coldstream' is now farmed by a son, J. Studholme, and interest in the garden is continued by his wife.

2. 'Westoe' is now administered by the Historic Places Trust.

3. Bulletin of the Dunedin Rhododendron Society, 1975.

larger gardens take shape

From the beginning of organised settlement in New Zealand there were men of vision, plant and tree lovers who, with their knowledge of the large English gardens, saw the potential in and took full advantage of the climate and soil of the new land for the making of beautiful estates. They were among the capitalists, the men with money and education whom Wakefield considered were necessary to the true balance of his ideal society. Their numbers included judges and lawyers, doctors and agriculturalists, politicians, and people from other walks of life, and they all had one thing in common: they planned and developed unusually attractive gardens.

In every area close to what became the main towns and cities, there remain a few gardens which were created by people of this calibre. In the country there are still large gardens about large homesteads and even where the homesteads have disappeared the fine old trees stand witness to the pioneer owners' love of their gardens, a characteristic which underlies the New Zealand way of life.

In those days a fine home was not complete without a garden, and as the population grew more substantial houses appeared and with them the landscaped garden. Many of these gardens were set in what were the most fertile areas and have disappeared with the development of suburbia. Others, now rated historic, have been added to the country's public gardens, such as Mona Vale in Christchurch, Isel in Nelson, and the Newton King garden at Brooklands, New Plymouth, while some, such as Glenfalloch on the Otago Peninsula, have been taken over by Trusts. A few are still maintained privately, the gardens restored to their former beauty and a source of pride to the owners.

Large private gardens have been established in modern times by people equally as interested in plants as were the early enthusiasts. The difference lies in the cost of maintenance – in those times a labourer cost about five shillings per week, whereas because of today's high labour costs many of the owners must of economic necessity do the work themselves. Social life in the late nineteenth century was simple compared to modern standards, and entertaining centred around the home. Garden parties and picnics were popular, and the large lawns and shade trees which grew so quickly and helped to soften the rather sternly ornate houses of the Victorian era with their high gables, towers and square outlines, were used to full advantage.

Trees were to play a very important role in the lives of the early settlers, orchardists, and particularly the farmers who needed them desperately for shelter. They were also required for replanting forests as timber was not everywhere available for housing. There was very little natural forest in Canterbury and by the 1870s what remained was being indiscriminately felled, the only area spared being Deans Bush at Riccarton where the Deans brothers settled in 1842.

Auckland was almost bare of trees because of eruptions in the past which had destroyed the forests of kauri leaving barren scoria over a large area, now city-scape and sprawling suburbia. The people who benefitted by the cry for trees were the nurserymen who were among the first settlers. A surprising number of trained gardeners set up their own businesses in shops and nurseries with little delay after their arrival in the first ships. They were responsible for stimulating interest in gardens and provided most of the vegetable seeds, fruit trees, and other economic plants that were the first requirement of most of the settlers. However, they did not take long to meet the steady demand for ornamentals. Their early lists reflect the fashions in England and the Continent for camellias, roses, fuchsias, peonies,

Opposite page. *Sun-filtering maples soften the brickwork gateway in the garden of 'Tupare', New Plymouth.*

2. *A large garden in which the gently undulating lawn is abruptly confined by mature deciduous trees. The character changes with the seasons and is reminiscent of the large English gardens on which it was probably modelled.*

3. *Bulbinellas border a path between formal and woodland gardens. These attractive herbaceous perennials flower in spring on stems half a metre tall. There are several New Zealand species, sometimes called the Maori onion.*

rhododendrons and azaleas, and many of the choice trees and plants that were being introduced to England by the plant explorers found their way to New Zealand, carried first by Wardian case, then by the end of the nineteenth century, in their dormant state by refrigerated ship. New vistas spread out before all those interested in plants and gardens as increasing numbers of exotic plants became available.

At first the nurserymen grew the quick, easily-grown hedging plants which were familiar to them; privet, broom, gorse, briar roses, thorn acacias, and particularly hawthorn which was produced by the million until it developed the fatal fire blight disease which was to threaten the apple orchards. Fruit trees were produced in enormous numbers but there was a vast expanse of empty country to develop. They found their way to Central Otago in the wake of the early gold rushes, and orchards appeared in every new province as it was settled. One early nursery which started in 1855 at Rangiora was that of Mr. W.E. Ivory. He "was particular in sending out the very best trees . . . and for a period of years they were recognised as a standard by which others could be judged. Ivory's Fruit Trees captured the trade of both the artisans and many of the settlers who were making homes for themselves."[1]

Quality became essential to success, so great was the competition in the South Island in such lines as fruit trees. Large established nurseries stocking general lines became familiar names throughout the country. Papanui Road, Christchurch, which contained some of the most magnificent gardens and finest homes in the country, now sadly cut up into suburban sections, also had the best laid-out nursery of any in Christchurch in its day. It was started by one Thomas Abbott, in 1872. According to Thomas Nairn, "He was a highly qualified nurseryman . . . very progressive in his outlook, and imported many new and rare plants. He also was wise in the choice of his men and had several very well qualified hands . . . his eldest son, Thomas jun., was an excellent plantsman."[2]

William Wilson, a leading Christchurch seedsman started a nursery and seed business in 1850. Robert Nairn, who was to become one of the leading nurserymen in Christchurch in the next century, recalls the extent to which Wilson's Nursery had grown by the 1860s, the largest in Canterbury. When he saw it in 1870, "It

was bounded by the following streets (now the centre of the city): Cashels Street, Manchester Street, Lichfield Street and Madras Street. Bedford Row was then the centre of the nursery, and down the centre was a green grass walk. At the entrance to Manchester Street there was a handsome pair of iron gates . . . and on the left a rather nice glasshouse filled with plants."[3] The whole of the block was in nursery.

About 1880 Charles Sontag, a nurseryman of German origin who had settled at Kaikorai, Otago, was growning tens of thousands of pines for shelter – *Pinus radiata, Pinus ponderosa,* the Austrian and the Corsican pines, *Abies excelsa,* and *Cupressus macrocarpa,* the Monterey Cedar,[4] that grand tree which grows so much better in New Zealand than its natural costal habitat of Monterey, California. In 1870 he advertised thousands of apples, plums, peaches, apricots, cherries and pear trees. But this was nothing compared to the insatiable demand that arose not long before the turn of the century when, with the development of the refrigerated shipping trade and the knowledge that fruit was as readily transportable from one hemisphere to the other as meat, a land rush started and orchards developed on a larger scale. Nurserymen avidly propagated fruit trees, importing new varieties from Australian and Tasmanian nurseries (for many years there was a reciprocal importation of trees and shrubs). Yet not all were content with 'bread and butter' lines that would provide them with an assured living. They had an eye for beauty, and they sold flower seeds and bulbs and a wide range of shrubs.

Opposite page. *Mona Vale, Christchurch, from the weir that raises a tributary of the Avon River to form the lawn-fringed lake in its restful grounds. This old home was bought by the city fathers to preserve it for posterity.*

2. *A woodland scene at 'Crosshills', typical of the English woodland garden which has been the continuing inspiration behind the design of its New Zealand counterpart.*

2

1

1 and opposite page. *A garden full of treasured plants was made by Mr and Mrs Bernard Hollard around their farm homestead at Kaponga. About two hectares has gradually been converted to a collection of plants of unusual interest, a feature being the massed plantings of groundcover foliage. The gardens are now under the scheme for garden preservation of the Queen Elizabeth II Trust, and are visited by many people who travel long distances to feel the atmosphere in this collector's paradise.*

Some of the catalogues are quite astonishing in the number of plants of all descriptions offered, but in all innocence they did import some plants that were to prove noxious weeds in the new enviromnent, such as gorse and broom seed, and honeysuckle and sweet brair. The latter, no doubt intended as understock for hybrid roses, was already running wild in the far north where the missionaries had used it for hedging.

Gorse, commonly used as a hedging plant in Scotland, soon clothed large hillside areas which had been cleared with the intention of sowing grass for grazing. It was a poor substitute, if a colourful one, in places like the eastern hills of Wellington which were covered with bush until 1840 when the first settlers arrived. G.F. Angas, an artist, described the early scene, "The harbour looks like a large blue lake embossed deep in hills. The green and umbrageous forest displays foliage equal in magnificence to that of the tropics."[5]

Paradoxically, the fact that exotics grew so well in the virgin soil of the new land also led to overproduction. Good times came and went swiftly, and when the demand slackened the nurserymen were often left with thousands of trees which they had to burn or sell by auction. This could well be the reason that many trees of one kind are to be found in certain areas, for most home gardeners then, as now, were susceptible to a bargain. Now large specimens, they pose problems in built-up areas.

Curiously enough, some of the large old trees which are landmarks on the west coast of the South Island, particularly around Greymouth, arrived there by a quirk of fate – a shipwreck. It was to be one of the biggest plant shipments for Australia, despatched from the New Plymouth nursery of Duncan and Davies. The ship diverted to Greymouth to load timber and went hopelessly aground on the bar at the river-mouth. What plants could be salvaged were distributed to local gardeners.

The export of trees and shrubs had reached quite large proportions by the beginning of the century and continued until after World War I when restrictions were gradually imposed which limited the free and easy passage of plants from one country to another.

There were also landscape gardeners among the pioneers. Although the first settler arrived in Dunedin only in 1848, by 1850 four nurserymen were in business there. One, George Matthews, who trained at the Edinburgh Botanic Gardens, was probably the first landscape gardener in the country. In 1866 another, Alfred Buxton, came to New Zealand and before the turn of the century had established his own landscaping business in Christchurch. He was to become the maker of some of the finest gardens, small as well as large, in both North and South Islands. Not trained as a landscape architect, he was responsible for some of the finest gardens throughout New Zealand and in his Christchurch nursery grew thousands of shrubs, trees and other plants for use in landscaping. He also employed a landscape architect, Edgar Taylor, to draw up his plans.[6] In 1946 Taylor was appointed to the Christchurch City Council as a landscape architect and was responsible for much of the replanning of the Botanic Gardens. Buxton moved his business to the North Island and continued to design and plant gardens on a smaller scale, but it is not known for certain whether he drew up his own plans or engaged Edgar Taylor for some very lovely gardens were created in that time.

The landscaping or designing of gardens in the 1870s coincided with several developments. Nurserymen and gardeners were making available a wide range of plants that flourished in the congenial climate and good soil, particularly in the warmer north. Labour was cheap and plentiful, and there was money in hand to employ skilled gardeners and men who had trained in the gardens of stately homes in England.

One who had been head gardener at the lovely 'Elmwood' estate in Papanui Road, and had laid out the landscape at 'Otahuna', Tai Tapu, for Sir Heaton Rhodes, was James Joyce, who started garden designing on his own account and had a considerable influence on the landscape scene in Christchurch. Many other experienced professional gardeners were to take the same course as demand for planned gardens grew. In the North Island it was difficult to escape the dominance of the English garden influence. Growing conditions encouraged greater scope for the imagination and embraced ideas gained from wider ethnic sources. More attention was also being paid to the use of native plants in association with the wide range of those from warmer climes.[7]

One charming garden on the slopes of Mt Egmont, near Kaponga, has a distinctly New Zealand atmosphere with its bush setting. It is a collector's paradise, Bernard Hollard and his wife having devoted their lives to their garden, sharing it with many people who visit them from afar. It contains a vast collection of mature exotic trees, shrubs and rhododendrons of which he has bred several named hybrids.

A real plantsman, Hollard has selected special forms of plants, including natives, and uses them well with a background of regenerated bush and many beautiful trees and shrubs, on hillsides and what were once swampy lower levels. The garden is at an altitude of 450 metres in a humid atmosphere and Bernard Hollard has made the best use of those plants that thrive naturally in the climate, using them in broad bands of colour as on an artist's palette, a delightful sight that attracts many tourists in spring. This property, which was originally part of a dairy farm, is now under the jurisdiction of the Queen Elizabeth National Trust, the aims of which are similar to the National Trusts of England and Scotland.

One of the most beautiful and distinctive gardens in New Zealand was once a rough-grassed and scrub-covered hillside on the outskirts of New Plymouth. It took vision and a lot of very hard work to carve 'Tupare' out of these raw acres, and after 50 years it is an ideal fulfilled for its owners, Sir Russell and Lady Matthews, who planned and created it together. The garden is now administered by the Queen Elizabeth II National Trust and is open to the public throughout the year.

The tudor-style house is set in the centre of a steep valley through which paths meander among the trees. Perfect specimens from the rare and unusual, the hardiest to the sub-tropical, evergreen and deciduous, thrive in the mild, sheltered climate. The collection of rhododendrons is outstanding but none of the trees or shrubs is grouped so that their botanical significance is greater than their direct effect in the complete landscape

'Mary Lane' is a winding pathway down the slopes beside a series of waterfalls set into a natural-looking rock garden. It leads to pleasant lawns and flower gardens and beyond, to the meadows beside the swift-flowing river on the boundary. Not many larger gardens today have developed so gracefully in the hands of perfectionists such as these.

Taranaki's fertile volcanic soil and humid climate is ideal for rhododendrons and they grow to perfection in the gardens of this province. On the eastern side of the North Island in line with Taranaki but divided by the high Ruahine Ranges, Hawke's Bay lies on totally different terrain. Its plains are often dry and bare in summer droughts, but green quickly after rain. In those areas that are closely settled, where water is available, the gardens are rich in plants that love the summer heat. The English trees dominate the landscape: the oak, the plane, the weeping willow hold pride of place, and autumn colour is superb. In the old farm gardens planes and elms still line the carriageways. In spring the blooms of peach and plum, pears and apple in commercial orchards dominate the landscape in sheets of pink or white. The oldest

'Tupare', New Plymouth, is famous for its beautiful garden with woodland walks, streams and a great diversity of hardy sub-tropical trees. The stream and bog-garden is a special feature.

One of the most outstanding gardens in New Zealand because of its unique character, it combines the best of the native fern species with the rhododendrons and azaleas ideally suited to the mild and humid climate. It could be said to have set the standard for the true New Zealand garden.

Opposite page. *The pool at 'Tupare'*

2. *A concrete arch frames house and garden.*

2

The tudor style home of 'Tupare' fits superbly into its garden surroundings, which are always a beautiful and breathtaking sight. The greatest impact is in September and October but the water garden is of particular interest the year round.

homes, once surrounded by large gardens, are found on the plains around Hastings to Napier, but few have remained in their original state. With the devoted first owners gone, they lose their identity though many of the old trees remain as landmarks. The 'hill' gardens at Napier and in Havelock North still retain some of their magnificence and sense of history, for these were the more recent retirement homes of the wealthy agriculturalists who made Hawke's Bay famous for its produce.

In the fertile region of the Waikato there are many notable gardens, some of historical interest. At Cambridge the huge old elms, oaks and beeches are jealously guarded reminders of the early days. As one ventures farther north, the pattern of gardening slowly dissolves into the sub-tropical, and there is an incongruous mixture of the hardy and the tender plants thriving together. In what other country could one grow palms and oranges successfully, beside the hardy deciduous trees from the northern hemisphere, as is commonplace around the Bay of Plenty, Auckland and the 'winterless' far north?

Some of the garden-minded settlers who bought land on the borders of the towns were attracted to their large plots by the natural beauty of the surroundings or the quality of the soil. What remains of their large gardens can be seen in such places as Epsom in Auckland, Lowry Bay near Wellington and Fendalton in Christchurch. Subdivisions are so small that many sections do not have sufficient space to retain a tree, but here special efforts have been made by some owners of new lots to retain some fine specimens, to the advantage of the general surroundings. Unfortunately the very beauty of many old established areas have been their undoing, making the retention of larger sections only affordable by the well-to-do.

In quiet country areas further afield farms are being broken up into smaller areas to cater for horticultural crops and the small farmer. This way of life appeals to younger city people who run a few horses for their family's recreation, or try their hand at self-maintenance farming in conjunction with a creative career in arts or crafts such as pottery, or producing specialised crops such as herbs. Some see in it the realization of a lifetime's dream in retirement, or an opportunity to bring up a family in a natural environment.

The remarkable colour of foliage and flowers and the landscaping with unusual and beautiful trees and shrubs attracts people to 'Tupare' all year round. This beautiful garden in New Plymouth is open to the public and is administered by the Queen Elizabeth II National Trust.

The making of Dame Cecily Pickerill's garden at Silverstream is in some ways typical of the large garden 'retreat' sought by professional people in the years between the Great Wars. Modelled on her husband's English background and created out of bare fields and mixed bush, this delightful garden is now an island of beauty.

The picturesque old-world house was built with local river stones and hand-adzed timbers. Rustic garden furniture is also hand-crafted and encourages outdoor living on the paved terrace.

In the 1920-30s there was a trend to buy tracts of several acres in the country as weekend hideaways, and many people bought these larger sections when they became available, including professional people who hoped to retire to a garden in the country. They spent what spare time they could to develop some very charming homes which are now on the outskirts of towns or in developing suburbs.

Dame Cecily Pickerill has one of the most charming larger gardens at Silverstream, in the Hutt Valley, which grew from this idea. Her pleasure, now in retirement, lies not only in caring for the garden but in the memories of its creation, the spare time devoted by her husband and herself, both plastic surgeons. She recalls the days when they gathered manure from the fields to improve the clay soil where giant rhododendrons now grow, and how the houses nearby are almost as plentiful as the mushrooms then; of loads of soil brought in to fill in the terraces and flower beds on the steep slopes, and of searching for beautiful stones to make a chimney on the cottage; of bringing back plants and other garden treasures collected on journeys abroad . . .

The early settlers who were garden minded chose their land for its qualities of soil or situation, never dreaming that the areas they selected would within a century become absorbed by town or city. Some of Dunedin's finest early homes and gardens have disappeared in this manner, and in Wellington massive flats and skyscrapers stand on what was the garden area of The Terrace, the street with one or two hectare blocks where the first well-to-do settlers built their solid new homes, carving gardens out of the bush.

Although the plans for Auckland or what was then the new capital were devised on the spot, they were little better than those drawn up in far-away England by the New Zealand Company for their towns, lacking imagination and vision, and being of the usual geometric grid design that inhibited any future change. But it is still the ugly basis for many suburban developments.

Auckland had great potential in the beautiful sprawling harbour and far-flung bays and inlets. At first her gardens were after the English tradition, its basic idea of tree-planting being just what the new capital needed.

Fortunately for the city, Epsom, the earliest garden area, still retains some of the fine old homes and many magnificent trees. The garden-minded people who made this part of Auckland so attractive included a man named Morton, Judge T.B. Gillies, Dr. A. Sinclair and G.B. Owen. The latter made frequent visits to Australia and returned with interesting plants. These men had magnificent gardens and employed several gardeners. They were apparently quite absorbed in the development of their estates. They were also responsible, with Sir George Grey of Kawau Island and others, for establishing the Auckland Acclimatisation Society which had a nursery at the Auckland Domain where plants and seeds imported from all over the world were raised.

Dame Cecily Pickerill's garden at Silverstream. The lower lawn as seen from the terrace of the home.

Opposite page. *Bluebells beside the house.*

The present Government House in Auckland stands among these early gardens in Epsom. In 1966 it was handed to the nation by Sir Frank and Lady Mappin whose home it had been for many years, but before that it had belonged to a man named Heather who bought the land about 1860 and spent 40 years developing the rough scoria-strewn hillside, part of the volcanic cone called Mt. Eden, its only apparent asset a glorious view. He shaped the hard terrain into terraces and scoria rock gardens, and created the spacious lawns enclosed by a well-planned collection of trees and sub-tropical plants.

Heather obtained many seedlings from his neighbours, Messrs Owen and Morton, including some unusual palms which gave the place an almost tropical atmosphere.

Sir Frank and Lady Mappin continued to improve the garden and their practical ideas included the planting of a single species for massed effect – forty plants of the bright red *Rhododendron griersonianum* alone occupy one terrace bed. In addition to brilliant splashes of colour such as this, they planted indigenous species – puriri, pohutukawa, and, under some of the rocky crags in the shade, king fern or *Marattia salicina*. The whole place has a typically northern New Zealand character. Containing the largest range of mature exotic plants to be found in a large garden setting in the Auckland region, it is indeed fit for a governor general's residence.

Opposite page. *Old stone steps at Government House gardens, Epsom, Auckland, which have been in use since the days of the original owners.*

2. *An old farmhouse at Waverley in Taranaki set in a large garden with many interesting facets. Azaleas, rhododendrons and other old-fashioned flowers grow here, among palms and deciduous trees.*

3. *The gentle curve of brick steps in a modern garden may take many years to mature gracefully. The 'newness' of this flight is plainly obvious when compared to the worn and established look of those in the Epsom garden.*

2

Auckland's warm, humid climate provided good growing conditions for sub-tropical fruits, and enterprising nurserymen encouraged their introduction. David Hay, who began a family business in 1855, imported and propagated trees and shrubs from California, France and England and Australia, and later specialised in citrus which were to become a profitable fruit in northern regions. It is of significant interest that one of the notable plantsmen with whom David Hay was associated was Luther Burbank, of California, and from whom he imported many now world-famous fruits, including the Burbank and Satsuma plums. Hay also imported other fruits from America, including the Delicious apple, Goldmine nectarine, and the Golden Queen peach, all of which are now household names. His influence in bringing into the country the unusual fruits such as the persimmon from Japan, is still felt today, at a time when there is renewed interest in the more exotic species for horticultural development for export and home gardens.

Norfolk Island pines were among the first trees to raise their symmetrical forms on the bare skyline of Auckland, and these were followed by the rounded shape of the glossy leaved *Magnolia grandiflora,* the feathery blue-flowered jacaranda, aromatic eucalyptus, and golden acacias. At one time a great many palms were introduced, and the mature specimens are one of Auckland's charms.

Port Nicholson (Wellington) was settled in 1840. The nearby Hutt Valley contained some of the finest soil for gardening that man could dream of and became Wellington's market garden for 100 years. Francis Molesworth who arrived in 1840, brought with him a steam engine which could be adapted to sawing timber or grinding flour, thus demonstrating the typical enterprise of many of the settlers. He developed one of the first farms in the valley and used to spend his spare time collecting native plants with his neighbour, Alfred Ludlam, who purchased Molesworth's farm when he returned to England in 1845 and developed it into what became early this century the famous Bellevue Gardens. Ludlam's own extensive garden was at Waiwhetu. He was one of the founders of the Wellington Horticultural and Botanicial Society and later, with Sir James Hector and several others, was responsible for having the town belt set aside and the Botanical Gardens laid out.

Opposite page. *Wisteria hangs from the porch and a rhododendron blazes in the garden at Waverley.*

2. *Wellington Botanical Gardens was founded by Alfred Ludlam, an early settler who was also responsible for the setting aside of the town belt.*

2

"Ludlam was a recognised plant enthusiast collecting new and rare plants from everywhere . . . he visited Christchurch on one occasion in the seventies and brought with him a bunch of lapageria blooms and exhibited them in Duncan and Sons' Seed Shop in Cashel Street, creating quite a stir among the local plant lovers."[8]

Thomas ('Quaker') Mason probably established the first large garden which was to become renowned not only in his own land but overseas. He arrived at Port Nicholson in 1841 and purchased a large block of land at Taita, one of the richest areas of the Hutt Valley, He and his wife were idealists and Quakers by religion. They had sufficient money to carry out their dreams, and they were both young – 22 years of age.

Mason's plans were interrupted by the Maori wars in the late 1840s but this was a brief interlude which he turned to good use. He visited Tasmania and returned with a large assortment of apple trees which, with other fruit trees, he used as the basis of a commercial orchard. He was friendly with Ludlam and they exchanged plants. Mason also set aside five hectares as a landscaped garden, and from the early 1850s for the remaining fifty years of his life he imported seeds, bulbs, shrubs, and trees from all over the world to develop what was virtually a private botanic garden. He was said to have had 250 named rhododendrons and 60 named camellias, many treasures from Asia such as tree peonies and a *Magnolia campbellii* which was believed to be one of the largest in cultivation anywhere in the world. He called his place 'The Gums', and although it has long been subdivided for residental purposes a few of the fine trees he planted are still there. He was a generous man who shared his treasures with other gardeners throughout the country. The heyday of the large gardens came at a time when skilled labour was available, land was comparatively cheap and there were few distractions. In the case of the large farm garden, labour could be diverted when seasonal activities were at a low ebb. There was usually a handyman to help with the simple tasks, and this enabled the gardens to be maintained at a fairly high standard, but, as in any extensive garden, a requisite to success was the devoted interest of the owners.

Times have changed significantly from the days of Thomas Mason and Judge Gillies. The large home garden of their day has its counterparts, but very few owners still employ gardeners. This has resulted in garden owners who are intimately involved in the raising of plants and maintenance of gardens in their spare time. For most who choose to do this, it is a relaxing way of living or of filling their leisure time, a creative hobby that offers great relief from the stresses of city life which the pioneers never imagined. In many ways today's serious gardeners are, at heart, much the same as those early pioneers, each contributing to the beauty of their environment and helping to preserve a precious heritage of the finest plants introduced to the southern hemisphere in the last 100 years.

Opposite page. *Many Dunedin gardens were once part of larger gardens and still retain some of their character and charm.*

2. Magnolia campbellii *was brought into New Zealand as a seedling by W.M. Mason of Lower Hutt and it flowered there for the first time in 1880. It is still one of the most favoured of garden trees, flowering in late winter, a glorious sight.*

1,2,3. *Early History of Horticulture in New Zealand,* Banks Lecture by Robert Nairn, Royal NZ Institute of Horticulture, 1932.
4. *Pioneer Nurserymen of New Zealand,* Allen M. Hale, (A.H. & A.W. Reed)

5. *Early Wellington,* Louis E. Ward, (Whitcombe & Tombs).

6, 7, 8. *Changes in the Canterbury Landscape,* C. Challenger, Annual of the Royal NZ Institute of Horticulture, 1974.

everyman's garden

The first organised settlement of Europeans in New Zealand was made at Port Nicholson just before the signing of the Treaty of Waitangi. The settlers were attracted by the plans of the New Zealand Company, behind which lay the vision of Edward Gibbon Wakefield whose ideal was the establishment of a well-balanced community comprised of people from all walks of life, from labourers to professional men of some substance.

The new venture was given such publicity in the few years before emigration started that a great many people, inspired by the glowing descriptions of the new country and the opportunities it offered, were willing to risk everything on the venture. Naturally enough, it appealed to both professional and amateur gardeners, and it is not surprising that the first call by the offices of the New Zealand Society offering workmen free passages was for gardeners, agricultural workers, and artisans married and under thirty years of age.

They set out with their families and goods and chattels in the first ships, arriving at Port Nicholson early in January, 1840, in the wake of the *Tory* which had been sent on an exploratory voyage to purchase land in the most suitable parts of the country. Although many of the more well-to-do settlers had paid for the right to select sections under the lottery or ballot system of the Company, they found on arrival that the land had not been surveyed. By an error of judgement they stopped first at Pito-one (Petone) at the mouth of the river which flowed through the rich Hutt Valley. Some of them elected to stay when the rest moved on to Thorndon where a survey for the future city of Wellington was in progress.

There was plenty of work for the gardeners. Some took up land on their own account, others tilled the crops necessary to the new settlement, and others were soon making gardens for those who were in a position to build their first homes. Class distinctions merged as "man and master toiled with equal energy and goodwill," as T. M. Partridge, one of the settlers, wrote on March 18, 1840, "Fustian [thick dark cotton] coats and thick shoes are very fashionable, and you would laugh to see officers, doctors and dandies digging, thatching and chopping with great frenzy. The climate is glorious and the country like a Paradise ... I carpenterise and carry logs and cook and go to the council without detriment to my gentility."[1]

There is no doubt that in spite of the preliminary hardships the prospects of the new way of life pleased those families who were for the first time able to anticipate the possibility of owning their own land, homes, and gardens, however humble. But conditions were at first certainly uncomfortable. Some families had tents, others had brought prefabricated houses with them, a few were able to live temporarily in wooden shelters hastily erected by the Company, but most of them had to erect temporary dwellings of whatever was available – from fern trunks and totara bark to sticks plastered with mud and roofs 'thatched' with flax or raupo reeds and laced with the flexible supplejack vines from the forest or 'bush'. These huts, or whares as they were called by the Maori, leaked so abominably that in wet weather it was not unusual to find umbrellas erected indoors.

These trials did not last very long, however. And nobody could claim, even taking into account the alarming earthquakes and the Maori-European Wars which delayed settlement in the North Island, that the pioneers of New Zealand ever endured the hardships and privations of, for instance, their prototypes in North America.

The original plan to make a city at Thorndon, later called Wellington, was adhered to, and the swelling population which numbered 600 by February, 1840, moved there and lost no time in

Opposite page. *A maintenance-free garden in a small area beside a townhouse.*

2. *Many of Wellington's original settlers lie buried in the garden-cemetery that now constitutes a small but fascinating part of the Botanic Gardens.*

3. *A garden in Parnell which complements a house typical of the first houses established in this suburb.*

setting up urban society as they knew it. The urban pattern has lasted to this day, with suburban sprawl resulting from the continual subdivision of good land so necessary to food production and gardens and from lack of vision in preserving the best natural features of the countryside.

Those who came to planned settlements and founded cities and suburbs throughout the country had their lives organised for them from the beginning. They were on the whole solid citizens, industrious and thrifty. Gardening occupied them as a necessity to raise vegetables for food, and the ease with which these could be grown was a great encouragement.

Around the early dwellings "small patches for gardens were being cleared in various spots; ruddy-faced, flaxen-haired children were playing near the door, and the whole thing made an impression of cheerfulness and content."[2]

John Pierce wrote on April 6, 1840, "Vegetation (growth) seems constantly to be going on. On our garden parsley grows in abundance down to nearly low water mark. The natives never think about the seasons. They never dig but take a piece of wood and root up the ground and turn over the soil, and if there are eight potatoes they take up seven and just cover the one over and leave it to grow."[3]

Before long the newcomers were to realise that their preoccupation with planting according to the seasons, more particularly in the north, was no longer important; in many parts potatoes could be grown the year round. By this time potatoes had become a staple item of diet for the Maori. Introduced by Cook but more effectively by the whalers and missionaries, it had proved a godsend in those areas where it was difficult or impossible to grow the more tender kumara which required a long-growing season. The first settlers were glad to buy potatoes from the Maori until they grew their own.

Also of Port Nicholson, R. R. Strang says, "We are now in all the bustle and confusion of putting up a house . . . it is situated about 600 yards from the beach commanding a most delightful view of perhaps as fine a bay as there is in the world, and the ground so rich and productive that although somewhat gravelly, peas which were sown last week were, in six days, above ground, and this is the last month of their autumn, and the seed was injured by immersion in the sea. The climate is indeed salubrious and delightful."[4]

It was an upside down world. Although they knew that the Maori recognised no definite seasons, the fixed notion that spring, summer, autumn, and winter must be defined according to European standards has remained to this day, but the climate is just as capricious as then and seldom keeps to the timetable expected of it.

The hilly terrain and the swamps about Te Aro (which disappeared when the earthquake of 1848 raised the area) were not conducive to gardening on any large scale, but a letter from Charlotte Godley who lived in Wellington in 1850, describes her own garden, "The garden is very pretty . . . with sweet briar, honeysuckle, white moss roses and other real English plants . . . and overrun with fuchsias which makes hedges almost. There is some kitchen garden too, with our own cabbages, horse radish and lettuce, and there are lots of watercress in a stream close by. What is a great matter here is that the place is well fenced in."[5]

1. *A typical small home in Northland of the 1930s era with a bright and interesting garden. Dahlias, Cassia 'John Ball' and flax are some of the plants on show.*

Opposite page. *A late nineteenth century house in Nelson, the garden of which complements it in colour and style.*

The Hutt valley continued to be the main source of food and later became an important garden region.

As early as April, 1840, horses were imported from Sydney both for work and pleasure. By March, 1841, roads had been constructed by the Company's labourers, including the road to the Hutt, which "afforded delightful rides, a curious contrast being presented by the macadamised causeway and the groups of workmen and wheelbarrows among the primeval forest and wild scenery which they penetrated. At the Hutt the clearings looked cheerful and promising . . . neat cottages and luxurious gardens appeared along the banks . . . the rich crop had induced many a doubting settler to clear some land and the axe-men had begun to be a large and important class."[6]

It is hard to believe that scarcely three years elapsed from the time in January, 1840, when the first settlers arrived to the time they had cut down much of the accessible forest and cleared large areas of land to sow wheat (unsuccessfully), vegetables, and grass on which to raise cattle.

In November, 1841, a Horticultural and Botanical Society was formed in Wellington, and the first Horticultural Show was held during the remarkably fine, dry summer which followed. Prizes were given for cabbages weighing up to 9.5 kg, for potatoes grown from the seed provided by the Maori, for turnips 48 cm in diameter, and for many other vegetables, and grains, for herbs, and for fruits such as strawberries, gooseberries, blackcurrants, cherries, and seedling dahlias and geraniums and the first apples.[7] Prizes were also awarded cottage gardens.

By this time the social life had settled down to that of the normal English town, and the theme was to be repeated in all the other settlements planned or assisted by the Company. The town or future city increased its business establishments, the people of means built larger homes, the cottagers gained more neighbours on the outskirts or future suburbs of the town, and the larger areas of land accommodated the first farms.

The houses in the towns were built on the squares and rectangles conceived by English planners who had seen nothing of the contours of the land. The buildings appeared plain, practical and ugly until they were softened by trees or flower gardens. Out in the country more of the homes were simple, pleasing structures with wide verandahs, which were an ideal design for the climate and the new country's more informal way of living. These houses seemed to nestle into the landscape, more often than not surrounded by the type of garden resembling in form and content the cottage garden of the old land with its roses, hollyhocks, perennials, annuals, fruit trees and vegetable garden at the back.

Wellington's first suburb was established in 1841 from "some land acquired by Messrs Watt and Wade . . . divided into one-acre and two-acre lots . . . sold off at the rate of £20 per acre. The purchasers were chiefly working men who worked at their patches of ground after the day's toil was over. And Wade's Town (Wadestown) soon boasted a population of 200 persons, whose neat cottages and smiling cultivations peeped from every nook among the picturesque hills."[8]

However, many gardeners preferred Nelson to Wellington as it offered a greater possibility of procuring good land. The Company made unsold sections in Nelson freely available to those unskilled labourers for whom they had not been able to secure employment. The new province, which at first included Marlborough, also attracted wealthy people who acquired large tracts for farms and sheep-runs. Plenty of land was still available for agricultural and horticultural purposes; the growing of hops and barley was one of the first ventures, and fruit and later tobacco growing were to become profitable industries.

A nurseryman named McVicar set up business in Nelson in 1844 and by 1850 was offering 30 different varieties of apples, plums, cherries, Moorpark apricots (still a popular variety), pears, grapevines, and many other fruits. Ornamentals were grown by another pioneer nurseryman, William Hale, who also grew a line of glasshouse plants to satisfy the Victorian passion for tropical 'conservatory' plants – a demand which was responsible for an early interest in home greenhouses, even if it was only a lean-to affair on the side of the house. In 1853 he advertised monkey

2

3

4

Opposite page. *Valerian, sometimes a weed in the countryside, sets off this old stone wall at Oamaru.*

2. *A Waikanae garden where the lawn extends to make maximum use of the road verge.*

3. *This suburban home in Ashburton makes similar use of the space right out to the street.*

4. *Flats at Tauranga, bright with geraniums and roses.*

1. *A mature maple on the lawn lends an exotic touch to this Christchurch garden.*

Opposite page. *Seed of the monkey puzzle tree,* Araucaria imbricata *was advertised for sale in 1853 by William Hale. It soon became a popular feature of the landscape but its sheer size 50 years on necessitated removal from suburban gardens. There are few left today.*

puzzle tree seed at 25 shillings per packet. This curiously prickly pine tree from Chile, *Araucaria imbricata,* was to become a popular feature of the landscape until the early twentieth century by which time their great size in the Suburban gardens necessitated their removal. There are few left today.

It was not long before the interest in some plants justified specialisation on the part of nurserymen and one of the first to branch out was Henry Budden, who had a nursery in Nelson during the 1870s. He acquired land at Riwaka and grew large acreages of bulbs, from daffodils to hyacinths and treasures from South Africa and Chile which are still sought-after today. His fields when in flower were a great attraction to visitors and he whetted people's appetites for bulbs by exhibiting them at flower shows all over the country and supplying them overseas as well. This nurseryman was one of unusual talents. Besides being a community-minded person serving on local bodies, he made time to write on garden subjects for local newspapers and was a talented artist, recording many of the flowers he grew in botanically accurate water-colours. When his gardens were nearly ruined in a disastrous flood, he moved to higher ground and carried on.

2

Taranaki with its fertile volcanic soil and humid climate made it easy to grow as great a range of plants as anywhere else in New Zealand. When the first settlers arrived from Plymouth, England, they found the Maori already growing peaches in the large cultivated areas around their pa. A whaling station was established at Ngamoto Beach in 1828 and although no credit is given the whalers for planting gardens, it is not impossible that they could have introduced them, for as Crozet knew, trees would spring up wherever peach stones were thrown down.

When times quietened down after the Maori-European Wars, the settlers built some of the finest homes and laid out gardens that merged with the bush. They were foresighted enough to declare the slopes of beautiful Mt Egmont a national park to preserve it for posterity. Their love of plants and gardens encouraged the horticultural industry and today it is the centre of many nurseries. New Plymouth is specially noted for its beautiful gardens.

Dunedin and Christchurch have strong horticultural backgrounds. Dunedin with its hills and gullies deserved a better plan than the early surveyors gave it. They placed the usual grid of squares upon what could have been a beautifully landscaped town which the Scottish pioneers hopefully envisaged as a 'little Edinburgh'. Strangely enough it had a similar climate to, if a little kinder than that of Edinburgh. The settlers could succeed with anything that could be grown at home, so they sturdily set about making their environment as much a replica of their Scottish background as possible.

When the first settlers arrived there in 1848 the hills were clothed in thick forests, but by 1849, as recorded by a newly established newspaper which printed gardening advice, "Monster Cabbages: A few days ago we had the pleasure of inspecting two monster cabbages grown by a Mr David Bower, the gardener at Pelichet's Bay. They weighed 56 lbs and 48 lbs respectively and were grown on virgin bush land. Another instance of the surprising fertility of the land in the neighbourhood is the fact of the same individual having grown long red beetroot weighing 21 lbs.".[9]

Before long the bush was felled, the virgin soil exploited to the full, and the bare land cheerfully replanted with the familiar plants of the northern hemisphere. The transition was slow but effective, and today Dunedin, like Christchurch, has a largely European atmosphere created by its trees, gardens, pleasant parks, and botanic gardens.

The gardens of Christchurch are outstanding in their English image; it can be truly said that the citizens are the most garden-minded in New Zealand. This is all the more remarkable in view of its discouraging beginnings. Although the surveys were made and the roads formed before they arrived in 1850, the settlers were confronted with an almost treeless plain where humid and cold winds blew from north-west and south-west and the soil was either sandy and gravel-strewn or swampy. There was none of the virgin soil or the bushclad hills of either Dunedin or the Hutt Valley.

Christchurch was a challenge to these people who loved gardens, and they met it by making one of the most gracious cities in the country, with the outstanding botanic garden of the southern hemisphere. They softened the hard, uncompromising squares of the surveyor's plan by making the most of the River Avon which winds its idle way through the city and suburbs, providing a setting for many of the most beautiful homes.

Opposite page. *A small vegetable garden at 'Coldstream', South Canterbury.*

2. *An easily maintained courtyard beside a townhouse.*

In some ways Auckland was different to all the other cities. Governor Hobson selected the Waitemata Harbour as the site for the new capital, and the whole business of purchase and planning was done on behalf of the Government by September, 1840. Again the official surveyor Felton Matthew missed a glorious chance to plan an imaginative city around the unique volcanic cones.

By March, 1841, when Hobson took up residence and the city was officially made the country's capital, the first sale of town sections took place. These realised £100 per acre, but many of them were sold again by speculators so prices rose with every sale. Sir John Logan Campbell, often referred to as the 'father of Auckland', was among the early speculators. He bought the large central area of land which he eventually donated to the city as Cornwall Park.

It is interesting to note that speculation of land in New Zealand started even before the first of Wakefield's settlers arrived. Members of the New Zealand Company's Society bought up the first ballots of land and resold at a profit as soon as surveys were completed in Wellington. Within the year, land bought at £100 was worth £300 and, in the case of town lots, £1000. Land speculation was in fact the only means by which the ordinary people could establish themselves financially. Land values have been inflated and depressed, yet the sale and the subdivisions of land have given the people in the suburban areas the opportunity to make their own homes and gardens and move on at a profit; speculation has by no means been the prerogative of the well-to-do.

In the 1940s the State started subdividing land for those who could not afford their own homes, with even worse results than the private subdividers. Valuable topsoil was removed when levelling the land, as in the Porirua area, and the most fertile market gardens in the Hutt Valley were chosen for high density housing, where established gardens with old trees were destroyed.

The early settlers, while slaves to tradition in some ways, were freedom-seekers in others. Seldom did they put their roots deep down and stop for generations in one place. Gardens were made quickly but on the whole were regarded as transient things, and trees were not usually planted for posterity. The exotic species grew so fast that man was just as likely to cut them down as to plant them. He did not discover that forest giants were not for home gardens until they outgrew their space; his choice followed his fancy. Most of the large exotic trees which remain are those planted in public parks or in established gardens around the large farms and stations.

Auckland was not settled by people from specially chosen walks of life, after Wakefield's theories, but by a wide cross-section of adventurers and colonists who gave it just that extra note of sophistication, worldliness, and colour which remains to this day. There were certainly plenty of gardeners, and because the area was naturally treeless they planted all they could – Australian eucalyptus which were readily come by, the more colourful jacarandas which were already favoured, and native trees which cost next to nothing and included the best: kowhai, rimu, pohutukawa, and kauri. The growth of trees was fast, and soon Auckland was softened in outline by billowing green, a feature of its landscape today.

The settler in most parts of the North Island had a far from peaceful start. The Maori-European Wars sent him hurrying from homes and farms in the Waikato, Taranaki, Auckland, and when he returned he was soon bedevilled with other problems. Some of the plants he had brought with him became his new enemies, and the insects that were hidden in them were to wreak havoc. How was William Lyon, who sowed a Scotch thistle seed at a picnic held on his new farm at Pito-one to celebrate St. Andrews Day, November 30, 1840, to know that it would be a sad reminder of his national day?[10] Thistles and thorns, briars and ragwort, shrubs, annuals and fruits like the blackberry were soon to become noxious weeds, so firmly entrenched that they were to lay land waste until modern chemicals caught up with them.

A town garden in Parnell, Auckland.

2

There were plenty of insects already in the country, night-flying moths and beetles which developed an appetite for new plants such as grasses and vegetables, for example, but the introduced insects also bred fast in the new environment. Caterpillars had reached plague proportions by the 1870s when they travelled in army formation across the middle of the North Island. One of the first trains to New Plymouth was actually stopped in its tracks by the hordes of slimy bodies that were crushed on the rails and causing the wheels to slip. Fields were denuded of grass, and it seemed likely that the farm animals would die. One can imagine what happened to the gardens.[11]

The native birds which so entranced missionaries and pioneers alike with their melodious songs were nectar-sippers and as such of no use in the control of capterpillars, so acclimatisation societies made a careful selection of insect-eaters with due consideration to the fact that they must also be seed-eaters if they were not to starve in winter, and prolific breeders. Hence the wholesale importation of sparrows and other birds which met these qualifications. After they had finished off the caterpillars the birds started on the crops, so it became necessary to control their numbers, but the melodies of the native birds were already replaced by the familiar warble of the thrush and the blackbird which followed the gardener as he dug his soil – just as they did at home.[12]

The acclimatisation societies also introduced game birds, giving trigger-happy men the opportunity to go out and shoot anything on the wing. They stocked the streams with trout for the fishermen and introduced opossums from Australia so that this land, so lacking in native mammals, could provide furs. But the opossums became disastrous enemies of the garden and remain a source of discouragement in spite of trapping and shooting. The rats which escaped from the ships of Cook and the early whalers were however one of the most disastrous introductions. Plants grew magnificently on virgin soil but the enormous cabbages and beet of the first gardens became hard to duplicate. Disease in the form of fireblight, which was introduced by the thousands of hawthorns

sold for hedging, struck new orchards, and large plantings had to be destroyed to halt its spread. The hedges were torn out and replaced. Privet, escallonia and eleagnus were poor substitutes, and gorse had already revealed its runaway nature, so barberry was planted because it had the same qualities of thorniness as hawthorn and was excellent for farm purposes. In time, it too ran wild. The home gardener often bought hedge plants because they were cheap and plentiful and he could not afford better ones; his hedge was often as uniform as his white-painted picket fence.

Fruit-growers were to have more troubles when woolly aphids attacked commercial and home orchards without discrimination, and, with the increasing importation of trees from older countries where there were many more serious pests and diseases, some control had to be exercised.

The intervention of a wise Department of Agriculture with restrictions and a watchful eye meant an inevitable limiting of the gardener's opportunity to bring in more new plants from overseas. This was what people like Douglas Cook of 'Eastwoodhill' and other plantsmen before and after him had foreseen. By bringing in all the choicest and the rare plants they could procure, the country was well-stocked with a remarkable range of exotic plants before the peak of control was reached, with port inspections, quarantines, and fumigations. So today's New Zealanders inherit a virtual botanic wonderland within the confines of their ocean-bound islands.

By the 1870s the settlements were growing, and, in the South Island at least, the farms, on which much of the country's prosperity depended, were thriving. In the gardens a formal

Opposite page. *Lapageria rosea, a choice and rare plant which was introduced and exhibited in the early days, is still treasured by modern gardeners.*

2. *A New Plymouth garden viewed from the street.*

period began, a period when there were fashions for certain plants, like camellias, roses, fuchsias, rhododendrons, and bright bedding displays of annuals and geraniums. Curiously enough this fashion has continued. Bedding plants, in spite of their labour-intensive cost, bring a touch of Victoriana to modern towns and cities.

One of the basic traditional features of the community was the Flower Show. It had been a quarterly event of social importance in Britain and it continued in exactly the same way in New Zealand. To hold a flower show it was first necessary to form a horticultural society, and as soon as sufficient people were gathered together, people who had homes and gardens, this institution was set up. It made a splendid common meeting ground, master and worker competing fiercely for the honours of having the largest apples or pumpkins, or the most beautiful dahlias or roses.

Gardening was a great leveller then as it is now, but the 'cottager' often proved as good a gardener as the man of means.

No flower show was complete without its official opening performed by someone of social importance, regardless of whether they knew a marguerite from a marigold, and the custom shows little sign of fading away.

The first horticultural society was formed in Wellington in 1841 and wherever settlements grew others followed quickly. Christchurch was one of the first cities to have a Beautifying Society which was formed in 1897 with the objective of tidying up the city, planting reserves and improving suburban streets by planting suitable trees. Ugly fences gave way to gardened boundaries and offensive signs disappeared. The society started a competition for the best garden as seen from the street, which had a remarkable result by arousing pride in the peoples' surroundings. The idea has proved successful in other areas where it has been copied. But the results were so outstanding in Christchurch that the competitions were extended to take in other kinds of gardens, including the entire home garden and the factory gardens, improving the image of Christchurch to its status as the garden city. During peak periods at competition and show time, the city's gardens are a great tourist attraction.

Christchurch. Pride in their gardens has been greatly encouraged by competitions for the best garden viewed from the street, small and large, even factory gardens. These were prize-winners.

An old-fashioned arrangement of flowers in striking contrast to the simpler ikebana style of today. Each of these floral creations was made by the New Zealand Floral Art Society.

The Canterbury Horticultural Society has held shows in the past and occasionally in recent times in the manner of the famous Royal Horticultural Society's famous Chelsea Show in London. It also publishes its own magazine, *The City Beautiful* which does much to link the garden clubs together and provide information to members. It has its own horticultural building which provides a central venue for meetings and shows. It was endowed by an American, John Templin, who made his home in Christchurch, gardening his hobby. Other buildings in Auckland and Lower Hutt owned and financed by their societies, are in constant use for horticultural purposes.

For many years the home gardeners had specialised in raising their favourite flowers. The cottagers and artisans in England did valuable work improving certain flowers, such as the auricula and the polyanthus, and the tradition was handed down to the gardener who emigrated. The conditions were better than at home; plants matured and set seed quicker, there was more space in which to grow them, and there were more species with which to experiment. Specialist societies seemed the natural outcome.

These grew in strength and drew interest away from the broader sphere of the horticultural societies, until now, meeting monthly and producing their own publications. They hold their own conventions and flower shows, meet other specialists, and attend conventions in the northern hemisphere as well as host international shows and competitions here.

New Zealand's National Rose Society organised the first international rose convention, which was held in Hamilton in 1971. Since then there have been world daffodil, orchid and chrysanthemum shows.

Membership of Horticultural societies is maintained to spark community participation, but the younger people interested in gardening only when they have their own homes, tend to be uninterested in social or competitive events like this.

With less working time, they have more to involve themselves with their families, and with smaller sections around their homes, they tend to take a more practical interest in supplementing their food with fresh vegetables and fruit. They take an even more serious interest in 'organic gardening', another name for what the previous generation called 'compost gardening', their dedication developed from concern for the value of natural resources to retain good health in an age of synthetics and materialism.

For those seriously interested in horticulture there are now opportunities for education and practical work that were undreamed of in the days of their parents. While specialisation is the new keynote to success in a horticultural career, there have been amateur specialists from the earliest days of gardening in New Zealand. Dedicated people, they come from all walks of life, their binding interest in one plant genus. They share, hybridise, select, and show plants and flowers, undoubtedly improving quality by this co-operation. Some of the country's best flower-breeders are amateurs. The range of specialist societies include those for camellia, rose, lily, daffodil, gerbera, iris, cacti and succulent, rhododendron, orchid, proteas, rock and alpine garden, dahlia, gladioli, bromeliad, fuchsia, and even a soil association.

There are also the women's flower arrangement and floral art groups, whose interests include the Japanese art of ikebana. Bonsai, the art of dwarfing trees also has a following.

Overseas honours have been won by camellia, lily, daffodil, gerbera, iris, rose, cymbidium orchids, gladioli, and rhododendron breeders. As early as 1892 William Martin, the nurseryman of Dunedin who specialised in rhododendrons and other choice trees and shrubs, sent to Kew Gardens a rhododendron plant he had raised, which when it flowered was something of a sensation. It was named 'Marquis of Lothian' and was regarded as one of the finest rhododendrons in existence.

The development of plant breeding, even by amateurs, resulted in recognition of the need for legislative protection of new varieties, and the first phase of a Bill to protect breeders' rights was passed by the government in 1974. Since then there have been further advances and controls to protect breeders and growers.

1. *The Victorians grew orchids in their conservatories and never dreamed that some would one day be almost commonplace. They did not know the potential of the cymbidium, now one of the most popular commercial and amateur species, millions of flowers being shipped to overseas markets and thousands grown in the backyards of amateurs. The picture, of an Orchid Society's show in a modern shopping mall, demonstrates the popularity of orchids today.*

2. *Many gardeners have their specialities and Jack Clark of Auckland grows and trains bonsai trees. The subject this time is* Cedrus atlantica *'Glauca'.*

1

1. *A New Plymouth street which has been highly praised for its colour, form and character.*

2. *A cottage garden at Waikanae.*

3. *Spanish style home and garden at Whakatane.*

4. *The people of Queenstown, aware that they are part of an important tourist centre, take much pride in presenting a good frontage to their homes. This owner has made the most of a steep bank by massing it with perennials and annuals.*

Edgar Stead, probably the most famous of all New Zealand hybridists, made a beautiful garden at 'Ilam', an old homestead site with a stream running through it in what became the suburb of Fendalton, Christchurch. He was an ornithologist of note but was to become much better known for his strain of 'Ilam' azaleas and rhododendrons. He was one of the first in New Zealand to successfully undertake serious scientific breeding from 500 plants he imported from the best English strains obtainable.

He was devoted to "breeding plants and waited day by day to see each flower open . . . one of the most thrilling and satisfying of pleasures. In most cases he saved only one plant each of his best Ilam varieties. Mr Stead does this work as a hobby."[13] However many of them reached the members of the Rhododendron Society, of which Mr Stead was president, to be grown on by them, fortunately preserving those rhododendrons which have become favourites in our gardens today: 'Ilam Violet', 'Scarlet King', 'Kaka', and the famous 'Ilam' strain of deciduous azaleas. His work on azaleas was developed to further excellence at Massey University by Dr J. S. Yates who improved the azaleas, and who is noted for his lilium hybrids which he raised on a large scale, achieving fame with some of the varieties he named.

Today 'Ilam' is part of the Canterbury University campus, and its gardens have been retained as far as possible, open to the public when the azaleas and rhododendrons are at their peak in November.

Specialist societies serve a good purpose in preserving plants which might be lost to cultivation; they do not always seek the new. History is often bound up with these plants. It is recorded that Busby, British Resident at Waitangi, planted camellias around the present Treaty House at Waitangi before 1840, and some old pink flowered plants remain there today. As early as 1865 Alfred Ludlam of Waiwhetu published a list of fifty different varieties of camellia available. Old camellias can be found near the mission sites and by the graveyards of the pioneers. They were one of the most loved of the early flowers.

Old roses also have their champions and Nancy Steen of Auckland wrote a book, *The Charm of Old Roses,* which aroused great interest in the subject and inspired many people to seek out the sweetly scented flowers or similar varieties to those first planted around the mission stations and early homes which she described.

The result was the formation in 1970 of another very successful specialist society, Heritage Roses New Zealand, with the purpose of growing in members' gardens as many of these historic plants as can be found. The New Zealand Rose Society has a National Rose Trial Grounds at Palmerston North's Dougal McKenzie Rose Gardens, at which New Zealand varieties and introductions from overseas are judged on their performance each year.

Among flowers originally grown for pleasure and now big export business are the durable cymbidium orchids, which during New Zealand's winter and spring months are flown to Europe, Asia, and the United States where they are out of season.

The orchid was always regarded with something like awe; it was for the experts or the wealthy. However, new scientific methods of propagation enable large numbers of plants to be produced cheaply, and varieties formerly too expensive for the common gardener are now within his reach. The cymbidiums in particular are very popular with home gardeners, grown outside in summer and under cover in winter.

Today people are much more aware of scientific influences, and the language of gardening includes more frequent use of botanical names. The nurseryman with his more descriptive illustrated labels and closer observance of botanical nomenclature has assisted the gardener's education in this direction. The extensive use of chemicals has also made the need for knowledge essential to their proper use.

The encouragement and education of gardeners started very early. The newspapers, which were established as soon as the settlers arrived in each area, included special garden columns with information to instruct the home grower and widen his experience by describing plants and cultural practices.

1. *A small and intimate garden which makes full use of the limited space.*

2. *This man's hobby is roses. In his back-yard is a raised bed given over entirely to the miniature variety.*

Opposite page. *A larger garden, well-planned, well-maintained, and offering colour the year round.*

J. W. Matthews, a horticulturist and professional journalist who was the first person to write garden articles for papers throughout the country, founded in September 1944 the first gardening magazine of any significance, *The New Zealand Gardener*. It stimulated interest in gardening by gathering together the knowledge of many other well-known gardeners, experts in their fields. This was during the Second World War, when there was a campaign for people to garden and grow their own vegetables so that all possible food crops could be diverted to the war zones.

The war years actually stimulated gardening. Education in the schools was expanded in 1946 to include horticulture, and by 1947 there were 22,000 children's school plots. Later, children tended their gardens at home on a class competition basis, and farm children were encouraged to grow field crops on the same scheme. This was also a quiet way of interesting and involving parents.

Now the emphasis has changed to encourage children to take an interest in native plants and to study the general environment. At a higher level, diploma courses in horticulture at both Lincoln and Massey Universities were established early in the 1940s, and in 1948 the establishment of a chair of horticulture at Massey and shortly after at Lincoln was a significant advance.

Landscaping and town and country planning were added to university curricula with the promise of a better planned environment for New Zealand.

Opposite page. *A home is given great character when designed around an existing tree.*

2. *A garden at Waikanae, designed by Alfred Buxton.*

3. *A country gardener's back door.*

4

The Royal New Zealand Institute of Horticulture, founded in 1923, has had considerable impact on the horticultural scene, providing one of the few links between higher education and the home gardener; it encourages horticulture as a career through its diploma examinations conducted in conjunction with the universities, holds conferences and produces an annual journal featuring authoritive articles by leading horticulturists as well as a monthly journal in which students participate.

Fou___ed in 1923 and granted its Royal Charter in 1939, it has bec___ ___e senior horticultural authority, influencing such me___ ___e Plant Protection Act and encouraging conserva- tio___ ___ble for administering the notable Loder Cup A___ ___ter an interest in native plants. The Institute is ___ ___ognises notable service to horticulture b___ ___ssociates of Honour.

___ral secondary schools were adding ___their curricula and pupils were able to ___certificate examinations to further their ___ith diploma and degree courses were ___dents eager to qualify in the diploma ___degrees in horticulture. For the first time ___ fruit, vegetables, ornamental crops, ___agement was raised to a status of dignity, ___economy. People who had been interested ___see a living in it, were willing to invest their ___or horticulture, or set to work turning it into ___rryfruit farms, flowers, nuts, sub-tropical fruits. ___d by the new quick methods of propagation, could be ___ exported as well as any other product of the land.

___pertise of the horticulurist, professional or amateur has ___effective in breeding or selecting plants which are among ___ntry's prime exports. The first kiwifruit *Actinidia chinensis* ___ught back from China after a visit there by a Wanganui ___olmistress early in the century. The feijoa from South America

CARLTON 8834

has been greatly improved by selection, as has the tamarillo and other sub-tropical fruits.

The scientist has become an important cog in the wheel of horticulture. Even the nurserymen have their own research centre at Massey University, for like other growers they have the challenge of world export markets which demand high standards, whether it be fruit, plants or flowers. The impact of modern methods has changed the whole pattern of commercial horticulture and the nursery trade. With greater scientific co-operation and research they have reached a pace of development which the average gardener can scarcely comprehend. Yet it has been to his advantage. Plants once beyond his means, rare and beautiful orchids and other choice subjects are now within reach through the quick propagation method of mericloning. We can also be assured of virus-free strains, and healthier plants. This is not likely to affect the enthusiasm for breeding or selecting one's own specialties, and it will not change the home gardener's ways to any great extent.

Horticulture has become one of the finest of outdoor occupations for men and women, who are almost equally involved in this way of life.

1. *Not much space to spare in this Parnell garden except a tub filled with geraniums and lobelias.*

2. *A formal entrance to a Parnell garden with white petunias complementing the architecture.*

3. *Fallen logs have been utilised as flower garden pockets in this garden at Ohakune.*

4. *This volcanic rock wall on a sloping section at Ohakune substitutes for a fence and continues to the road verge.*

The modern trend to '10 acre blocks' in the country has meant an increasing number of small estates with a few horses, sheep, and rural gardens. They are often owned by young families seeking more space to move in, sometimes for a degree of social isolation, and frequently by retired people wishing to indulge their horticultural hobbies to supplement their living, whether it be the growing of vegetables to sell at the gate or flowers for the market.

The majority of people who garden live in the suburban or country areas, but today's leisure time, greater mobility and higher wages, does not always encourage them to stay at home and tend the garden; they have wider interests. Some have weekend cottages, away from the city. The first 'whares' or baches came into being in the late nineteenth century, eventually being caught up by the spread of urban growth, and today situated farther afield. It is not unusual for these retreats, still with space to garden, to become retirement homes for their owners. They are often in the milder coastal areas or by the lakes, places of quietude where in later years one can for the first time develop and indulge a passion for gardening.

Many of the most beautiful smaller gardens are the creation of both men and women of the older age group. To them, the growing of vegetables has become an important way of supplementing their incomes, and the interest provided keeps them alert and fit.

Home gardeners in New Zealand have always been adventurous and individualists. They garden as they please, plant a shade tree even if they do not have the time to sit under it, put artificial birds or unbelievable pixies on the lawn if they so fancy; they can have a greenhouse, make a rock garden, or dream up a trendy barbeque where they can entertain their friends, if they want to.

No longer is it traditional for men to attend to the vegetable garden and the women the flowers, the divisions are no longer fixed, the modern idea being to share the pleasures and work among the family.

The people's role in caring for and preserving the environment has undoubtedly been encouraged by school gardening programmes, gardening writers, radio and television, compost enthusiasts, specialists, and horticultural societies. Today the New Zealander is slowly turning back to look at what is left of the country's unique flora and is becoming concerned with the responsibility to conserve it – he is at last becoming aware of the priceless heritage of native plants which he has nearly lost.

The magnificent bush which thrilled the early botanists because it was unique is still being gradually destroyed by the steady economic pressures. But fortunately interest in native trees has gained impetus so that indigenous plants can at least take their rightful place beside the showier flowers, shrubs, and trees from other lands, which have gained a dominance in our gardens.

Opposite page. *Springtime in a sandy beach garden.*

2. *Flax makes an unusual contrast against this modern home.*

3. *A small garden in Northland where the garden runs into the surrounding bush.*

4. *A state house in an industrial area of Invercargill which brightens the area greatly with mid-summer annuals.*

2

3

4

Opposite page. *A bright sunflower emphasises the picket fence and Victorian architecture among Wellington's historic houses in the Tinakori Road area.*

2. *Wide steps complement the rock gardens of this terraced hillside in Dunedin. Even the crevices in the steps are fully utilised.*

3. *Bedding plants, such as pansies, are often used to good effect in the small garden.*

4. *An interesting driveway with mixed exotic and native trees.*

1, 2, 3, 4, 6, 7, 8, 10 Letters from the early settlers were printed in the *New Zealand Journal*, London, 1840. These are recorded in Louis E. Ward's *Early Wellington*, (Whitcombe and Tombs, 1928). The council referred to by Partridge was the governing body set up by the settlers as there was no official government in the country at the time.

5. *Letters from Early New Zealand*, 1850-53 Charlotte Godley.

9. *Pioneer Nurserymen of New Zealand*, Allen M. Hale, (Reed).

11, 12. *The New Zealand Gardener* 1947, James Drummond.

13. *The New Zealand Gardener*, April 1948, Dr J.S. Yeates.

native plants in the garden

Favourite plants of the Maori were among those also preferred by the early settlers — the clematis, kowhai, kakabeak, pohutukawa, and kumerahou or golden tainui. While the Eruopeans were to cultivate trees and shrubs in their gardens, the Maori only occasionally planted them around their dwellings for what could be called aesthetic reasons, the kakabeak in particular being noted by Captain Cook and also the Rev. William Colenso. It was used for personal adornment by the women, who threaded the stems through their pierced ears and wore the red flowers, shaped like parrots' beaks, as pendants.[1]

Another plant involved in personal adornment was noticed by Lieut. Crozet of the French expedition commanded by Marion du Fresne when it stayed at the Bay of Islands in 1772. He remarked that, "some of the Maori women wore necklaces made of small very hard black stones of a fruit which I do not know." The only seed which fits the description is that of *Planchonella costata*, a coastal tree still found in the Bay of Islands and called tawapou or tawa-a-pou by the Maori. It is also found in the East Cape and northern areas. It was pointed out to Colenso at Tolaga Bay near Captain Cook's watering place, his guides telling him "in times past the seeds were used for necklaces."[2]

Apart from the seeds this tree has a strong spreading habit of growth and lustrous green, wavy-edged leaves which should make it one of the finest of coastal trees for milder regions, yet it is still only rarely found in cultivation.

The colourful pohutukawa was used by the early European shipbuilders in the far north where the timber was appreciated for its hardness, and its habit of flowering in mid-December caused it to be adopted as their Christmas tree by the first Europeans. The yellow kowhai was so well liked that it has come to be regarded as the national flower of New Zealand, the fern the symbol.

The native or indigenous plants comprised few with flowers of bright or spectacular colour, but the variety of green shades in the bush, changing all the time as new growth comes and goes, is extraordinarily beautiful to those who have been living with it for a generation or two and who have accepted it for their own. Not so the early settlers, used to the colours of autumn in the trees at home, who could see little of beauty in the green canopy. Much of the native flora of New Zealand is unique and this was its great attraction to the botanist, the newly discovered land arousing an enormous amount of interest and botanical exploration from Cook's day onwards. The greatest naturalists of that day were to know New Zealand well and describe its natural life, its vegetation, and geography to such a degree that both Maori and pakeha (European) are fortunate to have a record of a heritage in danger of being destroyed by the civilisation inevitably imposed upon it.

The time of Cook's scientific exploration of the southern hemisphere in 1769 coincided with the acceptance of the Linnaeus system of universal plant nomenclature. Dr Solander, who accompanied the expedition as botanist to Sir Joseph Banks, the great naturalist, was a pupil of Linnaeus. Thus the first plants recorded were given scientific names which are recognised to this day and used by modern gardeners.

The discovery of an unspoilt land with a vegetation which was largely endemic excited the curiosity of other expeditions, with the greatest botanists of the time following in the footsteps of Cook and Banks and naming many plants.

The French explored the Islands too, and d'Urville made particular note of some of the Maori names. Botanical specimens were sent back to fill the herbariums of Europe, especially the Royal Botanic Gardens at Kew, until by the end of the nineteenth century most of

2

Opposite page. *The mountains of New Zealand have much to offer in the extraordinarily wide variety of plants that grow between the tree line and the snow line. Here, in the Richmond Range, Marlborough, a vegetable sheep (Raoulia eximia) grows in close proximity to an alpine buttercup (Ranunculus insignis).*

2. *The kakabeak,* Clianthus puniceus *was discovered by Dr Solander who accompanied Banks on Cook's first expedition in 1769. He found it cultivated by the natives around their dwellings when he landed at Anaura Bay near East Cape.*

2

3

the flora had been scientifically identified. But it was the missionaries who were to record the Maori names for the plants.

The natives' knowledge of the uses of plants for food and healing and of their names for them was fortunately collected also by the historian Elsdon Best and by the Rt. Rev. W.L. Williams, Bishop of Waiapu (a son of the Missionary William Williams). The latter contributed largely to a list of nearly 1,400 Maori plant names drawn up by T.F. Cheeseman for his monumental classic *Manual of New Zealand Flora* first published in 1906.

The first missionaries on the whole were a simple, devout people chosen by the Church Missionary Society for their knowledge of agriculture and practical skills as well as their Christian devotion. They, too, were affected by the great interest in the natural sciences which was at its peak in their homeland, Great Britain, and in Europe in the eighteenth and nineteenth centuries. These men felt an affinity with Nature and God and some of them became, in the course of their religious work, involved with botanical exploration.

The mission stations in the Bay of Islands were the calling place of some of the world's greatest scientists and botanists, from Darwin to Joseph Dalton Hooker (later Sir Joseph). Hooker who became Director at Kew, was to be called 'the father of New Zealand botany' and in 1864 he produced the first *Handbook of New Zealand Flora* by arrangement with the New Zealand Government. He collected and botanised at the Bay of Islands for some time in the course of a scientific expedition to the Antarctic in the ship *Erebus* in 1841, and met William Colenso who took him to the source of many plant colonies. Hooker engaged Colenso to collect herbarium specimens for him and maintained close touch with New Zealand until his death in 1911.

Colenso came to New Zealand as a missionary-printer, and was responsible for the first Bibles in the Maori language printed and distributed to the natives. But he was already interested in plants and had taken notes of many species which he regarded as new on his visits to outlying tribes. About this time Allan Cunningham, colonial botanist for New South Wales, was one of the first to supply the Sydney Botanic Gardens with New Zealand plants, and

J.C. Bidwill who in 1839 sent the first collection of live alpine plants to Kew, also took large quantities of native flora to grow in the Sydney Botanic Gardens of which he was, for a brief time, superintendent. They suffered great hardships whilst exploring new regions, penetrating areas that even to this day provide mighty obstacles to hardy trampers. On the whole the botanists were not interested in collecting plants for gardens and it probably never occurred to them that they would have enonomic value, except those already known, such as the flax.

A few of the missionaries were interested in growing native trees, and James Busby, the British Resident, is recorded as growing pohutukawa and cabbage trees to shelter his grapevines and his fig plantation. At Grove Cottage next to the Mission house at Waimate, groups of puriri, kauri, and other native trees were planted by missionary George Clarke.[3] The Maori did not have gardens which could compare to the Europeans for they were a communal-living people, but they knew the native flora so well that they gave many plants special names descriptive of their uses or their association with legends, such as the lovely *Clematis paniculata* or puawhananga. This was the Sacred Flower or Child of the Stars, named for one of the first-born children of Rehua (the star Antares) and Puanga (the star Rigel in Orion), whose duty it was to indicate by means of the blossoms the coming warmth of spring. [4]

Opposite page and 2. *New Zealand's best known tree,* **Metrosideros excelsa,** *the pohutukawa, is frequently used in public places with dramatic effect – the abundance of its scarlet flowers makes it one of the most spectacular trees of the New Zealand flora.*

3. *The early settlers had little interest in the native vegetation, although a few species, kowhai and pohutukawa especially, appealed to them. Nowadays the kowhai is a favourite with all New Zealanders, so much so that it is generally regarded as our national flower.*

2

Before the coming of the European, the Maori people cultivated large areas of kumara and taro which were as much a staple part of their diet as fish and bird; they also planted large groves of karaka trees, *Corynocarpus laevigatus* for food, and these are now found in almost every region where the Maori made their pa or villages, the original trees still standing in southern places such as Waikanae and Marlborough. The edible part of the karaka is the handsome, prune-shaped, golden fruit which hangs on the trees in February. The kernels which contain a poisonous alkaloid were treated before use by baking followed by suspension in running water for a long period before being baked again. Karaka leaves were also used to make chaplets for mourning.

The cultivated crops of the Maori were little troubled by the weeds, insect pests, and diseases with which the Europeans were so familiar and which were unwittingly introduced with such devastating results. But the early Maori did find some of the native caterpillars a nuisance, especially a large one called hotete which attacked the kumara. The Maori used to burn the leaves of the kawakawa, *Micropiper excelsum,* or those of the kauri tree, making a smouldering fire the smoke from which was said to destroy the caterpillars. Colenso recorded that seagulls were occasionally tamed and turned into the plantations to deal with the pests.[5]

The Maori were natural conservationists. They allowed to be taken from the sea and the forests only such fish, birds, and timber as were necessary for their requirements. They had strict laws (tapu) to prevent destruction of natural resources on which they depended for their sustenance although they were known to have set fire to the vegetation when they required more land for food crops.

In some parts of the country they used fire to encourage the growth of bracken fern, for the roots of these were also one of the foods on which they depended. Bracken became the curse of the settlers for it followed their burning of the bush, often supplanting pasture.

It is now certain that the common cabbage tree, as most people call *Cordyline australis,* was not the plant cut down by Cook's men, to have its leafy heart chopped up, cooked and eaten (like a cabbage). What Cook selected for food at Tolaga Bay was the nikau palm, and it seems certain that this was the plant that provided his men with the necessary 'greens' to prevent scurvy.[6] The sailors would have known it as a 'cabbage tree' as they called every palm by this name, even the common *Cordyline australis* which grew thickly in every swamp and looked, to them, just like another palm tree.

3

Opposite page. *Clematis are among the most beautiful of all flowering climbers of the temperate zones of the world, and the finest of the white-flowered species is undoubtedly the New Zealand evergreen* Clematis paniculata. *Its starry flowers drape the bush canopy in great festoons in September.*

2. *Karaka leaves and berries were of great significance to the Maori of old.*

3. *The nikau palm, the heart of which was eaten by Cook's sailors when they arrived at Tolaga Bay, has a natural distribution as far south as Greymouth and Banks Peninsula. Contrary to popular belief the age of this tall and graceful palm cannot be determined by the number of leaf scars on its trunk.*

The common name was perpetuated by the European settlers although the Maori name for all *Cordyline* species was ti, which the missionaries adopted for it as they preferred to use the native names for plants instead of the European common names.

The stems, roots and new green shoots of the nikau palm were used as food by the Maori, as were the inner stems of the mamaku or black tree fern, and the berries or fruits of the hinau, which has flowers like the European lily of the valley tree, clethra. Cook's men also used the manuka to make an effusion (tea) from it to prevent scurvy. The settlers used ti tree branches to make brooms, just as they had used switches of birch in England for sweeping paths and floors and even roads. The koromiko and the kumerahou are to this day used by both races as herbal remedies and other species have been revived for this purpose. The early settlers had little interest in the native vegetation although they planted a few species with flowers or foliage that appealed to them — trees such as the kowhai and pohutukawa. The kauri which stood in its great forests in the north was given a place of honour by planting it singly as a commemorative tree to mark a special event. A remnant of the giant forests remains at Waipoua where they are a national monument.

The shrubby, golden-flowered kumerahou and the bright red kakabeak both became popular in gardens but the rest were scarcely noticed, the people preferring their roses, apples, grapes, and pines. A few of the early nurserymen who were also collectors of native plants grew them in their gardens, encouraging others to do likewise and stimulating some consciousness of their ornamental possibilities. These men included W.M. Martin and George Matthews, among the first of Dunedin's nurserymen. George Matthews' son had a specialist nursery of native plants in the 1880s which amounted to several hundred trees, shrubs, and other plants including the exquisite *Ranunculus lyallii*.

After the first days of settlement in 1840, a completely new era started. On the best side, the pace of botanical knowledge increased, with the French adding their discoveries made on Banks Peninsula. The name of Raoul, a ship's surgeon-botanist who wrote a fascinating illustrated book, *Choix des Plantes de la Nouvelle Zelande,* is commemorated by the genus *Rauolia,* which contains species beloved by rock garden enthusiasts. Many of the botanist's names will be familiar to gardeners in the specific names of such plants as the mountain flax, *Phormium cookianum* named after James Cook, *Cordyline banksii* after Banks, and the large-leaved *Meryta sinclairii* (or pukanui) after Dr Sinclair, the botanical explorer. But the original Maori names of many native plants are in common use among gardeners.

Colenso, who discovered the first pukanui, *Meryta sinclairii,* jealously guarded by the Maori as something sacred, was one of the few botanists to stride both centuries, his period of collecting covering 65 years and conducted mostly in the North Island. We are fortunate that the first botanists, like the missionaries, kept accurate diaries reflecting a true picture of the untouched nature of the country — these botanists of the nineteenth century including Dr Lyall, Sir David Monro, who studied the alpine flora of the South as Bidwill had done in the North, Sir Julius Haast, John Buchanan, and H.H. Travers who investigated the plants of the Chatham Islands and found the amazing giant forget-me-not *(Myosotidium nobile)* which has become a treasured plant in modern gardens.

1. Cordyline australis, *the cabbage tree, is distinctive to the New Zealand landscape.*

2. *Mountain vegetation provides a textural contrast in the garden of a specialist grower of New Zealand native plants.*

3. *Pukanui,* Meryta sinclairii *was one of the sacred trees of the Maori first noted by Colenso at Whangaruru in Northland. This is a variegated cultivar.*

Opposite page. *A cultivar of the cabbage tree* Cordyline australis 'Alberti' *which originated as a sport in a European glass house, has returned to New Zealand as a garden subject.*

Great advances were made in these times. Sir James Hector, explorer, botanist and geologist, who became the first director of Geological Survey and manager of the New Zealand Institute which was to publish much invaluable information about native plants, was one of the earliest champions of the preservation of mountain forests and other native vegetation. At a time when there were few influential men with foresight or understanding, he persuaded the government to set aside for posterity untouched, large, mostly mountainous areas of great scenic and tourist potential. These are today's 'tapu' lands in that they conserve the watersheds of the lower lands on which the greatest number of people farmed and made their homes. Along with some more recently added forest and coastal parks they are the basis of the country's playgrounds, where tramping, walking, hunting, skiing, rowing, and boating on lakes have become a way of life.

At the three points of entry into the Mt Egmont region, walkways have been made with easily-manoeuvered paths linking the hostels and circumscribing the mountain. In the case of Mt Egmont alone, it was the early settlers who banded together to provide funds for it to be set aside and who formed the Regional Park body. At Arthur's Pass National Park, on the route from Christchurch to the West Coast, there are walkways leading to alpine areas which are noted for their flowers in December and January, and there is also a garden containing a representative collection of the plants in the area.

These areas serve as a constant reminder of what so much of the land was like before it was destroyed by civilised man. Over the last decade there has been a remarkable change in attitudes, largely due to education, which has encouraged the growth of responsible bodies interested in putting forward many of their ideas on conservation, some with practical effect. The creation of a Ministry for the Environment within government is a most important move with some power, and with great influence in arousing the moral sense of duty to preserve environments.

Membership of such organisations as the Forest and Bird Society has grown high enough to become influential, and there are many other alert groups.

An outstanding move toward practical preservation was made with the establishment in 1977 of the Queen Elizabeth II National Trust by an Act of Parliament. The purpose of the Trust is to encourage the protection and enhancement of open space for the benefit of the people of New Zealand; open space being defined as "any area of land or body of water that serves to preserve . . . any landscape of aesthetic, cultural, recreational, scenic, scientific or social interest or value."

Its objective is the negotiation of open space covenants for the perpetual preservation of areas of private land left in its natural state, in a voluntary agreement between the Trust and the landholder. This means that some particularly choice pieces of land with historic associations, bush remnants, small lakes, and lands with special qualities of landscape, even large farm gardens of special interest, can be retained and maintained while they remain in private ownership. In this last respect it has some likeness to the very successful National Gardens Trust of England.

Not all of the areas in which native plants remain, protected for the purposes of enjoyment and education are in trusts, or parks, public or private. Realising that these were available to most people only for the limited duration of their holidays, and that others did not have the opportunity to see them at all, extensive collections of native plants have been made into attractive gardens in areas controlled by county councils, towns, and boroughs. They are situated in botanic gardens, such as at Christchurch where the Cockayne Memorial garden was established in 1937 to commemorate Dr Leonard Cockayne, one of this century's famous botanists and the first to write a book for gardeners, "The Cultivation of New Zealand Plants." In the memorial garden there is a rockery for alpine plants and borders of trees and shrubs. It was not the first native plant collection made within these historic gardens, however, for as early as 1875 two acres were given over to showing "that native plants could be cultivated and were equal to expensive exotics."

Alpine plants make up a remarkable proportion of the New Zealand natives.

1.   Nature tends her own rock gardens in the alpine regions where some of the choicest plants are not so amenable to cultivation.

2.   Chionacloa flavescens, *a mountain grass, is one of the most ornamental species for gardens.*

3.   *There are twenty species of raoulias in New Zealand, sixteen of which reach the alpine zone. They are all excellent ground-cover plants, sometimes covering huge areas of rocky high country. Some species are admirable plants in home rock gardens.*

4.   *The red bidi-bidi,* Acaena microphylla, *in a garden near Motueka.*

5.   Celmisia major *is one of the finest members of the daisy family but is confined to the sub-alpine slopes of Mt Egmont. It can be grown in cool-climate rock gardens and, surprisingly enough, grows particularly well in the Edinburgh Botanic Gardens in Scotland.*

6.   *One of the choice high alpine daisies of the* Celmisia *genus which is difficult to grow in the lowlands but is forever a challenge to home gardeners.*

2

Dr Cockayne died in 1934 and his grave at the Otari native plant museum is covered with the tussock grasses he loved. This garden in Wilton, Wellington has become a mecca for all those interested in native plants. Walter Brockie, another noted botanist and plantsman, became its curator in 1947 and added outstanding rock gardens and pools to the attractive scene. It was in his time that the pink variegated flaxes, hybrid hebes, and dwarf kowhai 'Otari Gnome' became notable features of the gardens.

Since Brockie, R.H. Mole has been curator and has increased the importance of Otari's plants by grouping them to demonstrate their potential in the garden and landscape, and labelling them with information which encourages the home owner to grow them in his garden.

One of the last remnants of the natural bush near Wellington city, Otari is situated at an elevation which makes it possible to grow plants from almost every region of the country and is invaluable for botanical study and research as well as a horticultural attraction.

2.   Pachystegia insignis *'Minor'*, *considered to be one of New Zealand's finest dwarf shrubs, is well suited to rock gardens with light soil and is easily propagated from seed or cuttings.*

Opposite page. *A mixed garden of native trees, shrubs and perennials demonstrates the adaptability and beauty of a careful choice for garden purposes at the Otari Plant Museum, Wellington.*

An outstanding collection of native plants with the emphasis on the flora of the Bay of Plenty area can be seen at Opotiki's Hukataia Domain. Four and a half hectares canopied by puriri (one of which was estimated to be 2,500 years old) tawa, rewarewa, and ferns, interested Norman Potts, a local solicitor who was also a noted amateur botanist. Potts dedicated 35 years of his life to developing this domain into one of the most interesting native gardens in the country, planting, virtually unaided, hundreds of species many of which have started to regenerate naturally. Every species, and there are over 700 of them, is labelled. Since his death his work has been carried on by a committee comprising many of the people whom he encouraged to grow native plants, and the garden receives hundreds of interested visitors each year.

Norman Pott's influence will grow with time for he shared his knowledge widely and encouraged enthusiasm for his hobby. He was not alone in his dedication to the preservation of native plants, and many other people have demonstrated this by establishing private collections or supporting public ones.

Private collectors in the early days played their part in adding to the knowledge of native species and those who lived in remote and unlikely places were quite important to botanists.

One of the most romantic stories of these men was undoubtedly that of Charles Traill, a keen and knowledgeable amateur botanist who was appointed the first postmaster of Stewart Island. He had a store on Ulva Island in Paterson Inlet, and kept a notebook on native plants growing in those parts and corresponded with Thomas Kirk, Government Botanist. He supplied him and others "with ferns and other plants, secure in Wardian cases . . . and shipped them off from Ulva after painstaking efforts of wrapping and packaging." His great-neice Sheila Natusch, a notable author and artist of botanical books, in an article about his life in the Wellington Botanical Society's Bulletin (Sept. 1981) quotes an article in the *Southland Times* of 1891 "written in flowery terms". . .

"The portion of Ulva selected by Mr. Traill embraces three beautiful bays, two of them affording perfect shelter for sailing craft. The business of the owner's life became the beautifying of his property, already most singularly favoured by nature. After years of labour and the exercise of consummate taste, the spot grew to be one of romantic beauty – a veritable piece of fairyland, which attracted visitors and was acknowledged by all to be the site of the island. It is well-known with what luxuriance flowers and shrubs flourish in the moisture and genial atmosphere of that favoured portion of Foveaux Straits. There the nikau palm was seen side by side with the arbutus and the fuchsia, the latter presenting a mass of blossoms . . . throughout the grounds were scattered, along with the most exquisite heaths, specimens of fine plants carefully collected from the North Island and the Chathams. While Mr. Traill was possessed of considerable and diversified knowledge, his two passions were botany and natural history . . . At his own cost he peopled Ulva with English song birds which added the last charm to his delightful retreat."

One of the best-known historical writers on botancial subjects, A.W. Anderson, a horticulturist of Scottish descent who was director of the Timaru public gardens, made an alpine garden at Lake Tekapo in which he grew some of the finest alpine plants of the southern mountain regions. Many other South Island gardeners are dedicated enthusiastic alpine plant collectors.

Hebe hulkeana *is one of the most beautiful of these favourite small shrubs. It comes from the rocky coasts and is one of the few native plants which requires an alkaline soil.*

The Pukeiti Rhododendron Trust has made full use of its hundreds of hectares of bush as a background for rhododendrons. The Waipahihi Botanical Reserve at Taupo has restored and collected native vegetation of the area. Both these Trusts rely on public support, providing strong evidence of private interest in conservation. The passion to collect the endemic flora died down a little when most of it had been discovered and recorded, but the interest in botany continues with some excellent botanical societies and native alpine and flora clubs actively studying and exploring, still finding the occasional new species or variety. Much has been done by recent researchers to clarify the names recorded by certain of the early botanists, like Colenso who was not always eccurate in his later years. These names and classifications sometimes puzzle the gardener who is beginning to learn and apply the botanical names of many plants as he increasingly uses them, but interest in the correct application of names, encouraged by Cockayne in his books, and others after him, is increasing.

Botanists employed by museums and horticulturists have added greatly to the records and have produced illustrated books which the modern gardener can understand and fully appreciates.[6]

By growing and propagating native plants to present them as neatly as any of the exotics, the nurserymen have greatly increased public interest in buying them, especially in the new forms with coloured or variegated leaves. Notable progress has been made in the development of flax. First hybridised by W.B. Brockie of Christchurch and Otari, they are a great advance on even the popular forms such as *Phormium cookianum* 'Tricolor' which has been grown in gardens for over a century. It was said to have been collected on a cliff face by a European but the Maori claim to have had it growing at their pa long before. The many new hybrids have been given such names as 'Pink Delight,' 'Dazzler' and 'Yellow Wave,' and are striped longitudinally with red, cream pink or green.

Colourful leaf forms of many native plants have been noticed since early days and have stimulated gardeners' interest as they have always had a bias toward colour. But many more have become available since they have been discovered in the wild or developed in cultivation, and they are much sought-after for landscaping uses. Some native plants have a curious tendency to sport variegated forms, and these when propagated and distributed by nurserymen are released under cultivar names.[7] In the *Pittosporum* genus alone there are about twenty that vary from the original green-leaved species. Outstanding examples can be found in the puka or pukanui, the lancewood or the pseudopanax, the karaka, and the hebes. There are also red and yellow-coloured leaf forms such as the golden totara and the red-leaved rangiora. The variegated parapara has become one of the most popular houseplants outside of New Zealand.

The pukanui *(Meryta sinclairii)* is one of the most outstanding foliage plants for landscaping, and Cheeseman's story of Colenso's discovery adds interest to it. It was growing as a solitary tree at Paparumu in the Whangaruru Harbour "and was not known . . . on any part of the mainland and must be considered one of the rarest species of the New Zealand flora. The Maori state that it exists on the Poor Knights Island."[8] Later it was found growing in abundance on the Three Kings Islands and the Hen and Chickens Islands and identified by Hooker. It is used today as a specimen tree, in parks and gardens, in all except the colder parts of the country. There is a beautiful variegated form.

Many of the more treassred plants of the Maori came from the islets, although some of them remained to be discovered later in the nineteenth century. The rare member of the bignonia family, *Tecomanthe speciosa,* a creamy flowered plant of unusual charm, was discovered by Professor Baylis of Otago University late in the 1940s. *Xeronema callistemon,* too, is one of the outstanding discoveries of modern times and is a treasured plant in gardens. Apparently the Maori did not know of the existence of this flaming flowered perennial which lay hidden on the cliffs of the Poor Knights Islands off the east coast of North Auckland until it was discovered by Dr W.R.B. Oliver in 1926. Even more recently Major Johnson discovered the red-berried *Elingamita*. A strong factor in

1. *The native flax,* Phormium tenax *was among the first plants to be transported and grown in Europe. Greatly used as an ornamental, the new coloured hybrids have raised it to a status of importance as a garden plant.*

2. *Pseudopanax 'Gold Splash' is one of the selected varieties of species generally called 'lancewoods', and which has become a popular garden plant. It is reasonably wind-resistant and adaptable to most soils.*

Opposite page. Tecomanthe speciosa *is an example of the plant which is extremely rare in its wild habitat but by bringing it into cultivation it is now within the scope of the home gardener. Its creamy tubular flowers appear in winter and it is a vigorous climber if kept under control by pruning.*

the revival of interest and growth of popularity of the native species is that whereas many of the most beautiful took years to reach adult flowering size and form from seed, they can now be propagated under modern misting methods from cuttings which mature and grow quickly to flowering size. Thus a long waiting period is avoided, but to say that all native plants are slow-growing is a general misconception.

Some native species have been deliberately improved by selection or hybridising for home garden hedging, such as the humble *Corokia,* a spindly coastal plant now highly regarded as a hardy hedge shrub, beautiful in its flowers, berries, and colourful leaf forms. The tree fern has always had a certain appeal to gardeners, and it too is being used for its landscaping value as are many other ferns. Even the native flowers, so small and inconspicuous as a rule, vary; the white manuka in the far north, where a particularly large pink flowered form was discovered by an Auckland plantsman, Captain Keatley, and named for him, *Leptospermum scoparium* 'Keatleyii'. It was a sensation at the time, but not so much as the small, dark red *Leptospermum nichollsii* discovered on a Canterbury sheep-run by a shepherd named Nicholls. A sprig of this flower was noticed in Nicholl's buttonhole by Robert Nairn, a Christchurch nurseryman, who, realising its potential, grew it and sent a specimen to Kew. It was eventually exhibited at the Chelsea Show where it won a gold cup and was bought for a large sum.

The humble white manuka, enemy of the farmer because it 2 invaded his newly sown pastures, yet so beautiful with its clouds of white about Christmas-time, is fast disappearing before man's herbicides. But the early discovery of coloured forms has brought it back in a new guise as one of the most popular garden plants. It was noticed and hybridised by a noted Californian geneticist, Dr Lammerts, who created exciting, brightly coloured, large double and single forms under various cultivar names, such as 'Red Damask'.

The Maori derived his food, clothing, and wood from the indigenous plants, but the settlers were curiously blind to the conservation of timber, and with the destruction of the kauri and the white pine, the totara and the rimu, many of the smaller trees, shrubs and flowers went too. It is the horticulturist who has rescued many of them. This happened in Australia and South Africa, and the fact that so many of the plants from these countries were introduced to New Zealand during the last 130 years has not only saved some species from near extinction in their own lands, but they have provided food for the nectar-feeding songsters of the New Zealand bush. Now the tui, the 'blackbird with the white cravat' as the French settlers called him, or the 'parson bird' as he was to others, is not an uncommon sight in gardens where these plants thrive in company with such trees as the honey-rich kowhai.

Our native flora has been cultivated in Great Britain for many years, the alpines thriving in the Botanic Gardens of Edinburgh. The commoner species, such as the hebes, are found beside motorways in California, where the pohutukawa and flax are also common in gardens. The flax is the most widely distributed native plant, being honoured in Japan, while on the little island of St Helena it was the basis of the main fibre-producing industry.

The circle is slowly turning. The eyes of the gardener are more comprehending as they see some of the beauty that is beyond the little flowering world he has created about his own home. As he adds more native plants to his own preserves, he inevitably looks further and add his voice to those of the conservationists who fully understand the dangers that still exist to our remaining natural flora, in spite of all the lesson of the past.

Opposite Page. *The leptospermums, tea trees or manuka belong to the myrtle family and in the cultivars offer some of the finest of flowering, hardy shrubs. This delicate pink manuka discovered by Captain Keatley in North Auckland is named after him,* Leptospermum scoparium 'Keatleyii'.

2. A collection of manuka hybrids at Christchurch Botanic Gardens.

1. From *Nga Ranga O Waipapa* Maori History and Legend of the Coastal Tree *Planchonella costata,* N.Z., A. T. Porter.

2. George Clarke, a missionary, arrived in 1831 and built Grove Cottage. He spent his retirement, from about 1850 to 1871, planting indigenous trees. See S.W. Burstall, *Historic and Notable Trees of New Zealand,* Forest Research Institute.

3. *The Cultivation of New Zealand Trees and Shrubs,* L.J. Metcalfe, (A.H. & A.W. Reed).

4. *The Maori,* Elsdon Best, (Polynesian Society).

5. Information from the Journal of the Wellington Botanical Society.

6. *Mountain Flowers of New Zealand,* Nancy Adams, (Reed). *Flora of New Zealand,* Lucy B. Moore and Elizabeth Edgar, (Government Printer). *Plants of the New Zealand Coast,* Lucy B. Moore and Nancy Adams, (Paul's Book Arcade). *The Oxford Book of New Zealand Plants,* Lucy B. Moore and J.B. Irwin. *Rock Garden Plants of the Southern Alps,* W.R. Philipson and D. Hearn, (Caxton Press). *The Cultivation of New Zealand Plants,* L.J. Metcalf (Reed). *Gardening with New Zealand Plants,* Muriel Fisher. *Native Trees of New Zealand,* J.T. Salmon, (Reed).

7. Cultivar: cultivated plant of one selected variety which has been vegetatively propagated or comes true from seed, and is named.

8. *Manual of New Zealand Flora,* T.F. Cheeseman (Government Printer).

gardens for the people

Parks and gardens have been a feature of every city and town in New Zealand since the early days. They were not included in the plans of the first settlements for the simple reason that in 1840 the concept of such places for the pleasure of the people was a totally new idea. What were called public walks were being set aside in some parts of England, but it was not until 1845 that an Act of Parliament enabled the local authorities to purchase land for parks and support them from rates. The walkways and parks developed into gardens laid out in the manner of the stately garden estates of England, and when public gardens were eventually created in New Zealand they followed much the same design.

Some of the early surveyors did set aside land for open spaces, but there was the more important business of making homes for the people who, when they had time and the resources, turned to beautifying their immediate environment.

Whereas in England the purpose of parks and gardens had been to improve the shocking conditions of the industrial era that had crowded people into ugly towns and slums, in New Zealand it was a conscientious effort to uplift the image of the new towns and provide the people with a pleasurable outlet for their leisure time.

One of the first reserve areas which was to develop into a true 'garden of the people' was in Auckland, where Sir George Grey set aside an 80-hectare domain in 1845. It was here that the Auckland Acclimatisation Society later in the century raised seedlings and young trees from all over the world under the watchful care of certain keen home gardeners. They included Sir George who was by that time out of the political scene and creating his botanical paradise on Kawau Island. The domain at one time had the typical Victorian aviaries of foreign birds and cages of monkeys, attractions in those days when a stroll in the park was a Sunday outing. With its drives, walks, and lawns it was the nearest to a Botanic Gardens that Auckland achieved, until the opening of the Auckland Regional Botanic Gardens in 1982.

The Auckland Domain is still close to the centre of the city and has all the amenities of sports grounds, open spaces and gardens, museum, enclosed winter gardens with tropical and cool greenhouses, and a magnificent, formal lily pool and forecourt adorned with tropical climbers and statuary. Some of the first trees to be planted, giant Queensland kauris, and various pines and palms make an outstanding skyline.

Now an inner city garden, nearby Albert Park was once a barracks for British troops, not being declared a park until 1870 when the soldiers were sent home and the land vested in the city council. Some gigantic trees over 100 years old give this place a maturity that makes it hard to believe that until 1840 the city was almost treeless.

The original plan for Christchurch city, drawn up in 1850, also included an area for a botanic garden, a government domain, and a green belt. The land was covered with the sand and gravel of the wandering Waimakiriri River and threaded by the weed-choked Avon, yet the Christchurch Botanic Gardens are the most outstanding in the southern hemisphere and the pride of a very garden-minded city. The story of its making is told in *A Garden Century* which was published by the Christchurch City Council in 1963 to mark the garden's centenary, one of the milestones of horticulture in New Zealand.

The tropical greenhouse and the magnificent formal lily pool in The Domain, Auckland. Between the two greenhouses of the Winter Gardens is a courtyard containing another lily pond in which the tropical lotus flowers luxuriantly. The gardens are open daily to the public, displaying an extraordinary and enchanting collection of equatorial plants.

The settlers who arrived in 1850, however, did not have time to think of public gardens, and it was not until 1864 that they turned their attention to what they had and the tremendous asset of the 200-hectare Hagley Park was realised. In that year the Canterbury Horticultural and Acclimatisation society was formed, and it was decided to establish a botanic garden in the Hagley Park area. This society undoubtedly had a considerable influence on the development of the gardens and the raising and distribution of thousands of trees for public bodies throughout the Canterbury province.

Personal involvement in the creation of public gardens is fairly commonplace in New Zealand and must have encouraged interest and pride in the communities. There are many people who can proudly boast that their forebears helped in the planting of Hagley Park, and others today are carrying on the tradition of planting for posterity.

Sir George Grey donated 100 young oak trees to the park in 1865, and others gave Norfolk Island pines and many different conifer species, and flowering shrubs such as rhododendrons. Although it was claimed at the time that the first Cedar of Lebanon brought into the country was planted in Christchurch in 1865, a tree of this species had already been planted by John Edgerley at Hokianga in the 1840s. But the exchange of seeds with other botanical societies throughout the world started in Christchurch during this period and resulted in many interesting introductions, including marram grass which was to be used so successfully and widely on the coasts to hold shifting sands.

The gardens went through their periods of success and trial in good times and bad, but a succession of fine gardeners and today's skilled superintendents and landscape architects such as Edgar Taylor have designed the formation of walks, lakes, rock gardens, rose gardens, and greenhouses. The trees planted by the early citizens have grown to perfect maturity and their wishes have been fulfilled, for in this southern country so remote from their homeland they did indeed lay the foundations of what is almost a replica of the English countryside.

Wellington, for all its geographical disadvantages, formed its horticultural society within two years of the arrival of the first settlers, and it was to be responsible for the formation of a botanical gardens fitting well into the hilly slopes and glades so characteristic of the new capital. There were some of the country's most prominent naturalists and politicians interested in seeing that the new city had its share of public gardens – men like Hector, Ludlam, and Col. Wakefield.

1 and 2. *The Christchurch Botanic Gardens established in 1863 is now the leading botanical garden in New Zealand and certainly one of the major gardens in the southern hemisphere. Special features include the water gardens and the nearby rock garden.*

Opposite page. *Wellington's early settlers had scarcely arrived before they chose and planned a site for their botanical gardens. It lies in the heart of a valley in the most thickly populated area of Wellington city and is a great asset to the capital.*

No two New Zealand cities have gardens which can be said to be a replica of the other. The nature of the gardens was dictated by the great variety of soils, climatic conditions, and the influence of early gardeners who brought with them their own ideas on landscaping and planting. Most of the early superintendents were men who had been trained as head gardeners on large estates or botanical gardens in England or Scotland. Thus each town or city shows the influence of their skill.

David Tannock, a young Scotsman who had trained at the Edinburgh Botanic Gardens, did much to improve the status of Dunedin's Botanic Gardens when he arrived in 1903, bringing the true concept of the purpose of such an institution to his new domain. He remained there till his death, improving the design, adding rock gardens, planting trees of botanical significance as well as those that reminded the people of home, and developing large areas for special plants such as rhododendrons. The latter now comprise one of the most important older collections in the country.

The Dunedin Botanic Gardens, as with many others throughout the country, relied on the support of its citizens. The Horticultural Society formed in 1854 not only had an influence on its formation but each year in late October sponsors a Rhododendron Day which attracts thousands of people to enjoy the spectacular sight of the plants in full bloom. Such special days are also observed by the Pukeiti Rhododendron Trust in Taranaki, and the Canterbury Horticultural Society hosts the special rhododendron and azalea days at 'Ilam'.

2

From the mid 1870s on, trees were planted in public places to commemorate some special event or occasion, such as the visit of royalty or other important personalities, and the parks, reserves, and other public places abound in these historic trees.

Kauri and oaks were most popular for this purpose, but at Dunedin there is a refreshing departure from the usual in the huge mulberry tree planted to commemorate the visit of actress Ellen Terry in 1914.

Parks and gardens were often donated to their cities and towns by civic-minded citizens. Sir John Logan Campbell's gift to Auckland of Cornwall Park, planned under his guiding hand, became one of the finest large recreational and pleasure areas in the city. Comprising over 120 hectares, it is roaded and landscaped with broad avenues in the style favoured by the great French architects, and the wooded areas are comparable with the gardens designed by English landscapers who created pastoral scenes of tranquil beauty. There are groves of trees of one kind ranging from native species – kauri, rimu, nikau palms, and pohutukawa – to deciduous oaks reminiscent of England.

People like Campbelll planted many native trees, and today in Auckland the number of indigenous species exceeds that of any other city or town in the country.

3

Opposite page. *Dunedin's Botanic Gardens are a blaze of colour at any time of the year but especially so in spring when the magnolia trees are in bloom and azaleas and rhododendrons rival each other in a natural woodland setting.*

2. *John Logan Campbell, the man responsible for much that was good in Auckland's beginnings, employed a gardener who had previouly been associated with the man who landscaped the Golden Gate Park in San Francisco. As a result Cornwall Park was styled in the same way. Cornwall Park today is part of the 'green belt' which is an invaluable asset to New Zealand's largest city.*

3. *Old phoenix palms at Logan Campbell Park, a central recreational area of considerable importance to the city's environment.*

4. *Acacia Cottage, Logan Campbell's original kauri cottage, which was built for him by the Maori at Commercial Bay in the days before Auckland was settled. It was moved to Cornwall Park in 1920 and stands there to this day.*

4

Whangarei was enriched by the gift of H. B. Dobbie in 1910 of an area of native land which is a backdrop to the city. Mair Park on the banks of the Hatea River commemorates Gilbert Mair, an early settler, and was presented to the city by his son in 1914.

Water has played a considerable part in the making of parks and gardens.

Pukekura Park in New Plymouth, with Mt. Egmont as a backdrop, is dominated by a lake. Wanganui is another city which has been garden-minded from the start, and it has its river. The Wanganui Scenery Preservation and Beautifying Society was founded in 1910 by three former mayors – Messrs A. Hatrick, A. C. Bignell, and Hope Gibbons. An area of land by the riverbank was planted with trees and called Kowhai Park by Lord Liverpool, a former Governor General who planted a kowhai at the opening ceremony. Later, James McGregor and others planted many trees and transformed the area into a fine park, the name eventually being changed to the James McGregor Memorial Park. Since then a succession of people have continued planting. The land was vested in the city for purposes "of providing pleasure gardens, and other means of enjoyment or recreation". The original board of the Beautifying Society members was dissolved when the city council took over. From the small beginning of a public-spirited action by some leading citizens, the park has become a wonderful asset to Wanganui.

Virginia Lake in Wanganui is a beautiful stretch of water with a curious story. The beautiful park close to the main highway on St Johns Hill is surrounded by pleasant walks planted with trees of which the red gums are outstanding when in full flower about February. At the time of the early settlers, creeping sand-dunes threatened the lake and for a while the water supply for the new town almost drained it dry. But the Beautifying Society came to the rescue. Members met on Thursday and Saturday afternoons and wielded picks and shovels to make the paths. At the north end of the lake there had once been a Maori pa, and the Maori members of the Society were particularly interested in developing the park, helping with the work and raising funds for its further development. Many means were employed to raise funds for impovements, one of which was a lakeside concert by a male choir "which met with much competition from the frog population". Even in those days the society had to contend with vandalism and many of the young trees they planted went missing.[1]

1 and 2. *The well-tended municipal gardens of Whangarei offer a peaceful haven for lunchtime strollers amid the hustle and bustle of the north's busiest city.*

Opposite page. *The Esplanade Gardens at Napier is one of the finest foreshore promenade gardens in the land, while the celebrated Marine Parade – all three kilometres of it – is lined with an imposing plantation of Norfolk Island pines.*

1. *An unusual formal approach, with cabbage trees in the foreground, to the facade of the old parliament buildings. The new 'Beehive' is in the background.*

2. *The rose beds in front of the Parliamentary Library.*

3. *The gardens of Parliament, Wellington.*

LORD AUCKLAND

2

Wanganui is particularly notable for its wide range of exotic flora. Since the early days it has had men who were interested in importing seeds of rare and unusual plants, especially those of Australian and South African species which flourish in the warm climate. The society had a nursery in which the plants were raised and used for their work, the surplus being distributed to garden-minded citizens. So many notable plantsmen were associated with the early tree-planting days, and Wanganui reflects their interest in the great range of trees and shrubs in the gardens there today. The red gums which line College Street and are so striking in midsummmer 'were brought to Wanganui by Mrs E. M. White at the end of the last century. She paid a penny a seed for them in Sydney'.[2]

Wherever one goes in New Zealand there is no small town without its public park or garden. Where the local authorities did not make one, private citizens sometimes acted on their own. The Memorial Park on the waterfront at Kaikoura was planned and planted by a woman who made it her life's interest, gathering whalebones to edge the paths which she lined with shells and planting salt resistant hedges to shelter her flower borders.

Private homes with lovely gardens which have come under the control of city authorities include Isel Park and Broadgreen at Nelson, Queen's Park at Invercargill, and Mona Vale at Christchurch. There are other places where the old homes have gone but the gardens are preserved for the people.

Percy's Gardens at Petone, near Lower Hutt, with an entrance off the busy motorway from Wellington to the Wairarapa, was once the home of an early settler. Now within the sound of the roar of traffic, there are pleasant lawns, gardens, and bushwalks where the tui can still be heard, and its greenhouses and man-made lake create a little paradise close to a busy industrial area.

3

Opposite page. *A statue of Lord Auckland looks out over Aotea Square, Auckland city's civic centre.*

2. *The Palmerston North esplanade is on the edge of the city, a wonderful source of pleasure and relaxation for the people. Buses frequently stop here for visitors to picnic on the lawn.*

3. *Palmerston North's square is a restful place in the heart of the city. Tree-lined gardens next to city centres are a haven for shop and office workers.*

Christchurch Botanical Gardens is justly renowned for its woodlands and lawns.

2. *An outstanding feature of Queenstown is the park that occupies the peninsula. Beautification of this government owned reserve began in 1866 with a pioneer storekeeper and flourmiller by the name of Bandix Hallenstein, who was responsible for numerous local benefactions. The old trees include sequoias, cedars and silver birches.*

3. *Ashburton Public Domain was one of the first gardens established by the early settlers with plantings commencing around 1880. It contains gardens, lakes, many old trees and sporting facilities for bowlers, cricketers and cyclists.*

As time goes on, some of the smaller public gardens reach historic significance, such as the one at Queenstown with its 10.5 hectares on a peninsula on Lake Wakatipu and its magnificent backdrop of mountains. Although this was planted on glacial moraine, and some of the huge boulders are a feature, it has some old trees dating back to 1866. Here are magnificent examples of oaks, the American fir, *Abies grandis,* redwoods and monkey puzzle trees, cedars, sycamores, silver birches, and many more deciduous species – a botanical collection which delights the visitors from other countries who pour into this tourist centre of the southern lakes district. The park is one of the few administered by the Tourist Department, although there are excellent examples of gardens around many of the tourist lodges and hotels throughout the country, both privately and government-administered.

At no time in history has the interest in planting the areas inside and out of public buildings reached such a peak as today. But probably the most significant trend is the planting of what can be called inner gardens within cities, the opening up of spaces to provide gardens where people can sit and relax during their lunch-hours, and where flat-dwellers can take a breath of fresh air and enjoy sunshine and flowers. These have extended the concept of parks and reserves into something more intimate, a part of everyday living providing natural beauty among the grey of concrete and the noise of traffic. Here is not so much escape as compromise; the areas about libraries and civic buildings have become open living space as well as a setting for the buildings.

The interest of city planners, architects, and landscape gardeners has been excited in new techniques and in plants suitable and tolerant to pollution. Native plants have returned to prove their vigour and adaptability in these challenging conditions.

Arbor Day, once a single day of speech-making and concentrated tree-planting, has been revived but a growing interest in conservation and replanting is reaching everyone as never before. Conservation Week in early spring is another planting celebration. Even children are taking an active interest in replanting bare spaces, in beautifying and reafforesting otherwise waste places. The extension of bush walks and national walkways throughout the country has greatly encouraged interest in the countryside and provided healthful exercise for young and old. More interest is being taken by civic authorities in planting and providing playing space, green areas and gardens in what were bare spaces within city and suburb. New projects such as planting the main highways throughout the country are scheduled for starting in 1983, and hopefully this will extend further until each district has replantings indigenous to the area so that the true character of the natural countryside can be appreciated by newcomer, travellers and citizens alike.

2

3

1. Story by W. Boothby, former superintendent of Wanganui Parks and Reserves.

2. *Wanganui's Trees,* in the Wanganui Horticultural Society's handbook to commemorate the centennial of the Society.

Opposite page. *The top of Queen Street, Auckland, is softened by the planted verges, medians and traffic islands that create a welcome and colourful contrast in all seasons.*

2. *Lower Hutt has extensive gardens in the centre of the city as well as the suburbs, and is never without its colourful bedding displays.*

3. *This camellia tree in the garden of the old colonial cottage at Pipiriki was planted in the early 1880s – about as old as the house itself.*

places to visit

New Zealanders are inveterate garden visitors. In the early days the home was the focal point for social occasions, and the garden was the setting for tea and garden parties. People thought nothing of travelling long distances over rough roads in gigs or wagons to visit gardens in other centres. Then, as now, there were places designed specially to attract visitors, and these were popular with families who would spend Saturday or Sunday afternoons admiring the flowers, the peacocks and the talking parrots, the aviaries and the monkeys in cages, and partaking of afternoon teas for sixpence.

Sometimes there were donkeys pulling carts or St Bernard dogs harnessed to little carriages for the children. Wellington had several gardens in the outlying areas which later became the suburbs. Ludlam's Bellevue gardens and Mason's gardens at Lower Hutt were famous. There are still plenty of gardens to visit, but the theme is a little more sophisticated. The pace has been stepped up; people can travel farther, faster.

Old homes, many of them surrounded by gardens and plants typical of the early days, have in their turn become places worth visiting. Those of any importance that have survived 100 years or more have been restored or saved from destruction by private owners or by the Historic Places Trust which has done a great deal to encourage interest in the new heritage. Many of these places are now open to the public, and they range from some of the old mission houses in the north to Dunedin's Larnach Castle.

Other homes and gardens are open only for a special period of the year or upon invitation. Private gardens are occasionally open to the public in support of some charity or when they are at their best.

'Ilam', for example, in Christchurch, is open to the public in November. Special days for the public are also held at such places as Pukeiti Rhododendron Trust gardens in New Plymouth, the Waipahihi Botanical Society's reserve in Taupo, and the Eden Garden Society in Auckland. Beautiful gardens which have been consciously planned to attract the public are to be found in many districts, a notable example being the Waterlily Garden at Waihi, which attracts thousands of visitors throughout the summer.

In these restless times, people find a solace in gardens that they find nowhere else. By sharing the quietude and beauty of these places, relaxing in the intimate atmosphere they provide, they feel for a while that they have had a small part in their creation.

2

3

Opposite Page. *Eden Garden, Auckland is vested in a private garden society which administers it and opens it to the public. Members have worked voluntarily to make this unique collection of plants what it is today. This is a garden which has no off-season and is open to visitors all year round. The pink foliage of the* Cedrella sinensis *appears in spring and is a striking note among the variety of evergreens.*

2. Another view of Eden Garden which shows the exciting variety of evergreen trees.

3. The outstanding collection of conifers near the entrance to Eden Garden.

Opposite Page. *Sweeping lawns at 'Tupare', New Plymouth, a special gem in a corner of the land noted for its many lovely gardens.*

2. *'Tupare', New Plymouth. Cypress contrasts with the weeping Japanese maple in the foreground. This garden is open to visitors.*

3. *This old-world garden is snugly tucked away at the back of the Waitangi Treaty House, on the site of the original kitchen garden.*

2

Opposite Page. 'Hurworth', in Carrington Road, New Plymouth, is the remaining farmhouse in a small community that was established in the 1850s. It was the home of Sir Harry Atkinson, four times premier of New Zealand. It is now cared for by the New Zealand Historic Places Trust.

2. 'Richmond Cottage', a good example of one of the original stone homes in New Plymouth, was moved to a central point in the city to make it more accessible to visitors. It was once a beach house of the Atkinson family.

154

2

3

Opposite Page. 'Ilam', now the site of the University of Canterbury, was already a large landscaped garden when it was bought by Edgar Stead in the 1870s. He planted masses of rhododendrons and azaleas on the banks of the River Avon and became one of the most famous hybridists of these plants.

2. Waipahihi Gardens at Lake Taupo, is owned by a private society which has restored the bush in the area, created walks and replanted some areas with rhododendrons and other exotics including rock garden plants. It is always open to the public and is a popular attraction for tourists.

3. The New Zealand Rhododendron Society has its trial grounds at Kimbolton in the centre of the North Island, where a lake is surrounded by a magnificent collection of species and varieties. The Society has a large and active following among New Zealand gardeners.

1. The Pukeiti Rhododendron Trust was founded in 1951 by a group of horticultural idealists who saw the opportunity to create a garden on the scale designed by some of the great landscape visionaries of England. To them it was an opportunity to encourage others to become interested in ornamental trees and shrubs of all kinds but particularly in the rhododendron which was their specialty. The voluntary work of many dedicated members has transformed a sub-alpine wilderness of bush and scrub into a place with its own character, combining colourful collections of exotics with the native bush. The beautiful snow-capped cone of Mt Egmont is a backdrop to the 364-hectare reserve which is open to the public at the peak of the season, although special visits can be arranged with the Trust's secretary.

3

4

2. 'Glenfalloch', an enchanting garden eight kilometres from Dunedin on the Otago Peninsula, was planted by George Gray-Russell in 1860. Mr Philip Barling acquired it in 1920 and spent his lifetime developing it to a stage of near-perfection. It became one of the showplaces of Dunedin, with its glades of rhododendrons and many fine trees – collections of plants unusual so far south because of the peninsula's milder climate – water gardens, and a fine rock garden. Peacocks were introduced to strut about the lawns and add to the atmosphere of elegance. These exotic birds still greet visitors to 'Glenfalloch'. The original coach-house, converted to a 'Swiss chalet' by Mr Barling, has become a restaurant, and the garden and old homestead are now administered by the Otago Peninsula Trust and are open to visitors for most of the year.

3. Thomas Marsden arrived in Nelson in 1842. Within six years he had settled at Stoke where he built 'Isel', a solid home of good design, and planned a garden in a setting of the trees he loved. When Marsden died in 1926 the estate was acquired by the Nelson City Council which has preserved the home and maintained the garden. 'Isel Park', as it became known, is now greatly enjoyed by all the people of Nelson as well as visitors from afar.

4. 'Crosshills', a sheep station in the crisp air of Kimbolton, in the southern central North Island, is famous for its rhododendron garden of 15 hectares. Created out of the undulating farmland surrounding the homestead it consists of collections of thousands of rhododendrons, landscaped with the emphasis on colour grouping and the natural divisions of the genus. Associated with deciduous trees and conifers, and traversed by broad mowed walks and hillside paths, it reaches a peak in October and November. At that time it is opened to the public and visited by thousands.

1 2.and 3. 'Mona Vale', Christchurch, is now owned by the city council and has become in recent years a centre for social events. The garden is partially retained by specialist societies, the plantings by the Iris Society in particular providing a spectacle of great beauty in spring.

1. and 2. 'Broadgreen' at Stoke, is one of Nelson's oldest established homesteads. Built of cob (rammed earth) for one of the early settlers, Edward Buxton of Derbyshire, it has stood the test of time. The interior has been restored and furnished to suit his period and the garden is notable for its stately trees and large formal garden.